TENNESSEE PERSONAL INJURY

A STEP-BY-STEP GUIDE

TO YOUR PERSONAL INJURY CASE

FROM CLAIM TO TRIAL

- 2017 EDITION -

WRITTEN BY

STEVE D. KARR AND JAMES A. FLEXER

© JAMES A. FLEXER, STEVE D. KARR, FLEXER LAW 2017. ALL RIGHTS RESERVED.

ISBN: 978-0-9977853-1-9

All Photos Used by Permission from Pixabay.com under the Creative Commons usage license.

Edited by Christina Rado

The material contained herein does not constitute legal advice. The information contained herein does not indicate an attorney-client relationship. This book is intended to provide accurate and authoritative information regarding the subject matter covered. This book should not and cannot substitute for the independent judgment and skills of a competent attorney or other professional who has examined your particular situation.

TABLE OF CONTENTS

FOREWORD 2
INTRODUCTION: FOUR INJURY SITUATIONS 4
TYPES OF NEGLIGENCE CASES 8
MEDICAL ISSUES 8
MEDICAL EXPENSES YOU MAY INCUR 12
LOST WAGES AND CAPACITY TO EARN 14
PAIN AND SUFFERING AND LOSS OF ENJOYMENT OF LIFE 15
TYPES OF DAMAGES 17
PROVING LIABILITY OR RESPONSIBILITY IN YOUR PERSONAL INJURY CLAIM 21
MOTOR VEHICLE COLLISIONS: AFTER THE ACCIDENT 22
A NOTE ABOUT INSURANCE COMPANIES AND SOCIAL MEDIA 28
SLIP AND FALL ACCIDENTS 32
DOG BITE CLAIMS 36
DEATH CLAIMS 40
GOVERNMENTAL NEGLIGENCE 45
CASES INVOLVING FEDERAL, STATE AND COUNTY GOVERNMENTS 46
AFTER YOU HAVE FINISHED MEDICAL TREATMENT 49
INSURANCE RESERVES 52
YOUR DEMAND LETTER 53
I CAN'T SETTLE MY CASE - WHAT NEXT? 57
WHERE SHOULD I FILE MY LAWSUIT? 60
ADDITIONAL RESPONSIBLE PARTIES 63
THE TRIAL – GENERAL SESSIONS COURT 67
THE VERDICT 72

THE CIRCUIT COURT CASE	74
ONCE EVERYONE IS SERVED	78
WHAT IS DISCOVERY?	79
INTERROGATORIES	81
SAMPLE QUESTIONS YOU MAY BE ASKED (INTERROGATORIES):	81
INTERROGATORY SAMPLES TO SEND TO THE DEFENDANT:	83
DEPOSITIONS	87
THE DOCTORS' DEPOSITIONS	89
MEDIATION	92
PRETRIAL MOTIONS	95
EVIDENCE IN TENNESSEE: BASIC RULES	96
THE TRIAL – CIRCUIT COURT	104
POST TRIAL MOTION AND APPEALS	110
SUBROGRATION AND SETTLEMENT	112
CONCLUSION	114
APPENDIX A: SAMPLE DEMAND LETTER	115
APPENDIX B: GENERAL SESSIONS WARRANT – SAMPLE	118
APPENDIX B: GENERAL SESSIONS WARRANT – SAMPLE	119
APPENDIX C: CIRCUIT COURT SUMMONS – SAMPLE	120
APPENDIX D: CIRCUIT COURT COST BOND - SAMPLE	121
APPENDIX E: CIRCUIT COURT SUBPOENA – SAMPLE	122
APPENDIX F: GENERAL SESSIONS SUBPOENA – SAMPLE	124
APPENDIX G: JURY VERDICT FORM - SAMPLE	126
INDEX	127
ABOUT THE AUTHORS	129

FOREWORD

By James Flexer, Founder and Owner of Flexer Law

We would not have written this book if we didn't have to. However, after spending a considerable amount of time looking for an informative, easy to understand guide to the basics of personal injury law in Tennessee, we came up empty.

Granted, there are numerous excellent books about personal injury in general, and texts on Tennessee trial techniques and procedure, but we could find nothing suitable to fill the need for a clear, accurate, and up to date book on Tennessee personal injury for everyone.

Like so many areas of law that are so specialized, what to do if you are injured is something you don't give a lot of thought to… until it happens. We hope you take from this book a clear understanding of when you may have a legal case for an injury and how to properly handle it.

With this in mind, we have written *Tennessee Personal Injury* with the goal to make it easy to read and understand, while revealing some of the lesser known and understood issues in a personal injury case in Tennessee.

Finally - a book about Tennessee personal injuries written for you. We hope you enjoy it and feel more confident of your control of the situation if you are ever involved in a personal injury that was someone else's fault.

James Flexer
July 2016
Nashville, Tennessee

INTRODUCTION: FOUR INJURY SITUATIONS

You are driving on one of Tennessee's highways. Suddenly, without warning, you are struck by an 18-wheeler. Your vehicle is sent out of control and hits a guardrail. You are petrified - sore and bruised. You may have suffered from broken ribs or broken bones. You have never been in a collision before - you don't know what to do.

You walk into the grocery store looking for the frozen foods section in the grocery store. You have already placed some items in the grocery cart you selected upon entering the store. As you are looking for the frozen dinners, your foot hits a small puddle of water and you hit the ground in a violent fashion. You are in pain and feel your right ankle begin to swell. The store manager takes down your information. After you have gone to the hospital and a few days have gone by, you call the store's claims department and give them your information. No one calls you back - you don't know what to do.

You allow your 11-year-old boy to go play baseball at his best friend's house. The friend's mom is there at the house, but she gets preoccupied with a TV show. The boys start getting wild and mom is not supervising at all. Your son gets accidentally hit in the head with a baseball bat and has a concussion and a very serious head injury. After your son is rushed to the hospital in an ambulance, placed in intensive care, and after you've signed a bunch of forms at the hospital that you were too stressed to fully read and understand, where do you start to pick up the pieces and deal with the unthinkable?

Your family member is driving on a local roadway early one Saturday evening. As they approach an intersection, another vehicle speeds through the stop sign, hits your family member's vehicle broadside, doing thousands of dollars of damage to both vehicles. Your family member is unconscious and taken to the local hospital. Due to the massive injuries suffered, your loved one is air lifted to one of the major hospitals in the city. The life-threatening injuries require surgery. For two days, they lay in the hospital until death becomes imminent. Your family makes the decision to take your loved one off life support. Your family is devastated and does not know where to turn for help - what should they do?

Four different situations - all of these have one thing in common. They are all what we call personal injury cases, or in the legal profession, cases involving negligence. There are several things you must prove in order to recover. More important for your purposes, you must prove that an injury occurred, was caused by the action of the at-fault party, and you must prove damages.

What are you allowed to recover? Basically, you are allowed to recover all medical expenses that are related to your accident. In the event you have an automobile accident, you will recover the ambulance bill incurred after being involved in the collision. Of course, you will recover the emergency room bill after being taken to the hospital or medical center. If you need additional related treatment, those expenses should be recovered as well, and could include X-rays, CT scans, MRIs, and physical therapy, etc.

Suppose your doctor tells you that you will miss work? Well, you are able to recover your **lost wages**. This usually means from the date you are laid up from the accident until the time you are able to go back to work. If your injuries are so severe that you can't return to your job doing some type of work, you can recover for **loss of capacity to earn**. This is generally very difficult to prove unless your injuries are severe or incapacitating and your doctor has given you an excuse for this long period of time.

The other major element of recovery is **pain and suffering**. This is very difficult to determine. Obviously an injury involving a fracture or disc herniation to the neck or to the back will involve more pain and suffering than an injury which heals within a few weeks or months of the collision. Nevertheless, pain and suffering is real and <u>**you**</u> are entitled to recover for it.

Remember the loved one who was killed by the driver who sped through the stop sign? This case involves negligence as well and is generally referred to as a wrongful death case. Aside from recovering all medical expenses from the date of injury to the time of death, the family can recover for the loved one's funeral expenses, pain and suffering from the time of accident to the time of death, and the economic value of the loved one's life.

In the next several pages, we will explore in some detail what it takes to put together <u>**your**</u> personal injury case, the types of cases involved, the damages involved, and handling the case from start to finish.

TYPES OF NEGLIGENCE CASES

Here are a few of the types of negligence cases usually seen by most trial attorneys. They are as follows:

1. Motor vehicle collisions
2. Slip and fall (premises liability cases)
3. Dog bite cases
4. Wrongful death cases

We will discuss each of the above cases in this book in detail. There are also certain special types of negligence cases which are seen in the legal profession. Not every negligence case fits into the round hole or square peg.

MEDICAL ISSUES

If you have been involved in an automobile collision, the first thing you should do is be examined by a medical provider. Injuries may take time to develop. It may be a day or two before you begin to feel any pain, especially in your neck or back area. A "whiplash" or soft tissue injury is usually painful and can be nagging in nature. If your pain is ongoing, do not wait. The insurance company will doubt that you sustained an injury if you don't get treatment very, very soon. *Don't delay!*

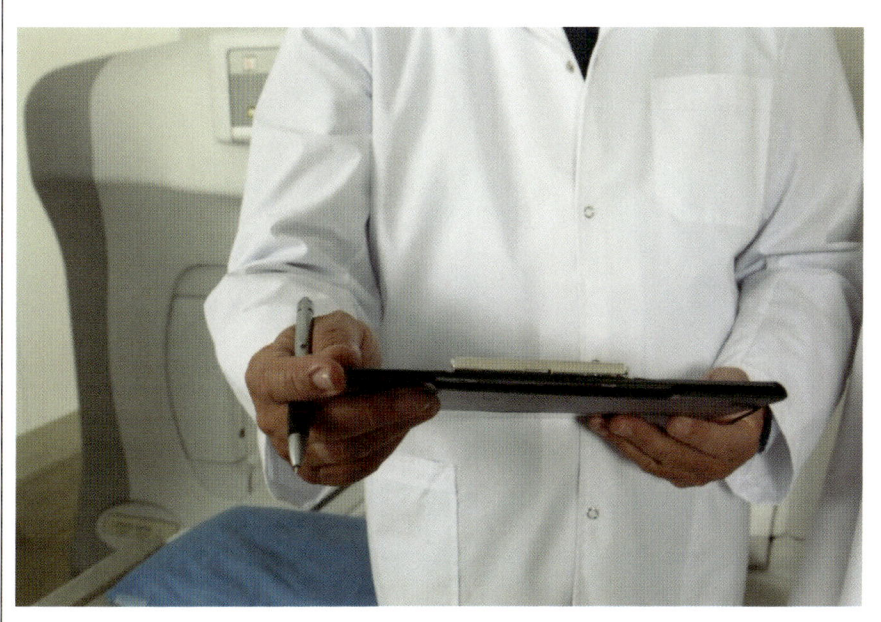

If you have been injured in an accident, be sure to seek treatment immediately! Failure to seek treatment soon after the accident can potentially make your injury worse and can even hurt your case.

Do not forget that you may have what is called **medical pay** (med pay) coverage with your automobile insurance. **You generally have to use this before your health insurance will pay for any of your medical bills related to the accident.** If you are a Medicare recipient, you must exhaust your automobile insurance medical pay coverage before Medicare will pay your bills. Be sure to check your automobile insurance policy to see if you do have medical pay coverage as part of your policy.

Sometimes health insurance will not cover injuries sustained in a negligence or personal injury claim. This could put you in a very tough spot because you have no way of paying your medical bills except from your own pocket. There may be resources available to you which allow you to obtain treatment on what is called a **lien**, which is an agreement that the doctor will treat you now and wait until the case is settled to receive their payment from your case's proceeds. Unfortunately for the injured person, these resources are usually only available if you go through an attorney. The good news is that you do not have to pay the doctor/hospital up front and do not have to pay the medical provider back until the case has been resolved. Over time, the number of these medical providers who accept liens has grown and there are a number of quality medical providers who are able to treat your injuries. Don't avoid getting the necessary care for your injuries just because of money. You will only be hurting yourself.

Pre-existing medical problems that have been <u>aggravated</u> by someone's neglect are damages you can recover. Most of us of a certain age have experienced neck or back pain. Some of us have had to seek medical attention over our lifetime. Even if you have had previous neck, back or shoulder surgery before, do not be discouraged - you still have a claim!

There is one important thing you should know. Always be honest with your medical provider. If you have had a previous problem with any body part, whether it be by accident or otherwise, share it with your medical provider. This is important because the provider must be able to say that your injury was caused or aggravated by the accident. If your provider can say this to a reasonable degree of medical certainty or probability, your claim is much stronger with a higher likelihood of success.

MEDICAL EXPENSES YOU MAY INCUR

Injuries in a motor vehicle or other personal injury accident will generally involve a number of medical bills. Initially, there could be an ambulance or EMS (Emergency Medical Services) bill for transporting you to the local hospital or medical center and treatment on the way. Once at the medical center, you will encounter the emergency medical physician(s) and nurse(s) who will examine you and diagnose your injuries. There will be blood tests, blood pressure checks, breathing tests, heart checks, and the list can go on and on depending on the injury. You can probably expect X-rays to determine whether or not you sustained any fractures (broken bones). Depending on the severity of your condition, there may be more advanced testing such as MRIs or CT scans. These tests detect injuries involving soft tissue and/or disc herniation in the spine. If you leave the hospital without being admitted, you may be given a prescription for pain or muscle relaxers. There may also be instructions to follow up with your personal physician or a specialist. It is best to fill your prescriptions at the earliest possible time.

If you see a specialist, you will incur their medical bills as well. You may see an orthopedic doctor, a neurosurgeon, a neurologist, or a chiropractor, etc. You may also see a physical therapist, who will try to help ease your pain with various exercises and the like to improve what is known as your range of motion (the ability to move your neck, back, etc. comfortably). Several physical therapy sessions can cost quite a sum, so be prepared for that as you recover from your injury. Treatment with a medical lien for payment may be an option, meaning the medical provider agrees to treat you now and wait until your case is over to be paid, thereby placing a lien on your anticipated settlement money.

Hopefully your injuries will not require surgery. If, however, this is the case, there will be numerous large charges. Aside from the surgeon's fee, there will be hospital charges, anesthesia charges, and charges for various equipment, just to name a few. Depending on the type of surgery, you may encounter physical therapy again. Obviously, there will be medication for pain as the first days after surgery can be quite painful.

Medical expenses are a major part of your recoverable damages. You should keep track of your providers on your own. A qualified personal injury attorney will work to keep track of all medical providers you have seen for your injury. You should keep a list of all the medical providers you have seen as well as copies of all of your medical bills to share this information with an attorney should you choose to hire one.

LOST WAGES AND CAPACITY TO EARN

Another of the elements involved in your motor vehicle or personal injury case is your **right to lost wages**. Following your injury, or in the event that you need surgery following the accident, your doctor could require you to be off work. In that event, it is extremely important that you obtain an "out of work" note from your doctor. You should retain one for your records and make sure your employer obtains a copy. This is the best way to document that your doctor has kept you off work. Each time you see the doctor, you should obtain an "off work" slip again, keeping a copy for yourself and giving a copy to your employer. Once you have recovered from your injuries and return to work, make sure someone who takes care of payroll can document the hours you were off as well as the rate of pay. This will determine the dollar amount missed from work as a result of the injuries.

Loss of earning capacity is another element closely related to loss of earnings. This is a little more difficult to prove. Not only would you need proof from your doctor as to your ability to work, often experts may need to be consulted as well. Occupational experts and economists could be needed to determine what kind of work you could do in the future and how much your loss of capacity to earn would be. These experts can be expensive to hire but a qualified personal injury attorney knows these experts and can assist you in proving this form of damage.

Both loss of earnings and the capacity to earn are important parts of your case and are not to be overlooked.

PAIN AND SUFFERING AND LOSS OF ENJOYMENT OF LIFE

The element of damages most difficult to prove is pain and suffering. It is difficult because there are no hard numbers or figures you can use to prove this amount. Obviously, medical expenses and lost wages are easy to prove because there are hard numbers associated with these elements. Pain and suffering is hard to determine; however, lawyers are able to estimate what a jury might award depending on the county where the case would be tried.

One way to determine your pain and suffering is how the accident has affected your life. How has the accident affected your ability to enjoy activities you enjoyed before the accident? Some of us are avid sports lovers and love to play the game; some of us love to dance; some of us love to go to the movies, cook, or garden as hobbies. The accident may have prevented you from doing these things permanently or on a temporary basis.

*Has the accident prevented you
from doing the things you love?*

How about taking care of your personal hygiene? Bathing and showering can be difficult after sustaining injuries by accident. Combing your hair or shaving could cause problems for a period of time. Walking down stairs or riding your bike could be quite painful. Also, doing chores around the house may prove to be just too difficult.

All these things we are talking about are things we take for granted every day, especially when we are unable to do them for a short period of time or even permanently. This can be quite upsetting. At some point, the emotional toil and stress may express itself in irritability, insomnia, depression or some other psychological or psychiatric illness.

You are entitled to something for your pain and suffering. Depending upon the severity of the injury, this could be a sizeable part of your damages.

TYPES OF DAMAGES

Nominal damages are recoverable when there has been a violation of legal rights but no damage. An example would be the rear end collision: you are stopped at a red light and are rear ended by the driver behind you. There is no damage to your vehicle nor did you sustain any personal injury. Technically the driver who rear ended you was negligent and you could sue for negligence. Since there was no property damage nor was there an injury, the judge could award $1.00 in damages because there was a technical violation of the law – but no damage. In other words, the judge is granting a symbolic award to you.

Nominal damages are important where a Tennessee or United States law is providing your theory of recovery; if nominal damages are established, then attorney fees can be awarded to your attorney. Consumer protection laws and laws protecting your civil rights allow attorney fees if nominal damages are granted. The recovery of attorney fees will encourage attorneys to pursue a case where the actual damages are small, but an important public policy (consumer rights, civil rights) is being protected.

Compensatory Damages are damages designed to compensate you for injury and medical expenses you sustain. There is no fixed formula for these damages and are left up to a judge or jury to decide. Compensatory damages are divided into two categories – economic damages (you can place a dollar amount on them) and non-economic damages (these are more intangible damages and don't have a monetary value). Compensatory damages are awarded for the following:
- Medical bills – economic damages
- Loss of earnings – economic damages

- Loss of earning capacity – economic damages
- Pain and suffering – non-economic damages
- Loss of enjoyment of life – non-economic damages

In Tennessee, recent laws have been passed which limit the award that the plaintiff can recover from the defendant in regards to non-economic damages. Non-economic damages are currently limited to $750,000 per plaintiff. In the event a plaintiff suffers a catastrophic injury such as paraplegia, amputation, burns or wrongful death as a parent of minor children, the cap is increased to $1,000,000 per plaintiff.

Punitive damages are granted in order to punish the wrongdoer. These are awarded when an act is done willfully or maliciously or in reckless disregard of the plaintiff's rights. An example of this would be the driver who gets behind the wheel of an automobile, truck, boat, etc. when they are intoxicated. When this occurs, it puts pressure on the insurance company to offer more money than they ordinarily might in a case of mere negligence.

Loss of consortium means the loss of the love, affection, or society of one's spouse. Simply put, if a husband or wife is injured as a result of another person's negligence, the other spouse has a right of action which is derivative in nature. The loss of consortium would not exist but for the negligence of the wrongdoer. This term can mean many things. An example would be the spouse could not help with chores around the house for a period of time. The spouse may not be able to go on long walks like they did before the accident. The couple's sex life may have been affected by the personal injury. As a practical matter, the loss of consortium claim does not have great value unless the spouse has been severely injured or has tragically been killed as a result of the accident.

In Tennessee, loss of consortium has been extended to the loss of children wrongfully killed and to parents wrongfully killed. Such benefits include the loss of affection, guidance, care, protection, training, companionship, and love.

PROVING LIABILITY OR RESPONSIBILITY IN YOUR PERSONAL INJURY CLAIM

In every claim for personal injury, the person seeking damages must prove liability (responsibility) of the person or entity who is alleged to have caused the damages. In a motor vehicle accident, the first piece of information needed is the accident report. This report can be obtained by going to the local investigating authority (police department or highway patrol). Should you hire an attorney, the attorney's office will usually obtain the report for you.

The accident report gives you quite a bit of information, as the officer is required to take down a number of observations and facts about the accident. Of course, you will have the names and addresses of all parties involved in the collision. The make and models of the vehicles involved will also be part of the report. The officer should obtain the names of all insurance companies who insure each of the parties involved. More often than not, the officer will draw a diagram of what happened after speaking with all parties who were involved or any witnesses. Finally, the officer generally will make some comment as to what he or she believed to have caused the collision.

MOTOR VEHICLE COLLISIONS: AFTER THE ACCIDENT

After you have gotten over the initial shock of having been involved in a motor vehicle accident or other traumatic event causing injuries, try to remember a few key points.

With an auto or truck accident, make sure you or someone calls 9-1-1 to document the accident. Make sure you cooperate with the police officer and be sure to have your vehicle registration and your insurance information nearby. Also, try to remember to take photographs of all vehicles involved if you have a cell phone with you so that you will have documented proof of the collision. **Make sure you do not make any statement on the scene that might lead one to believe that you were at fault in any way.** If your vehicle is unable to be driven from the scene, you will be in need of some form of transportation. Be sure you know where they are taking your vehicle

Though you may not want to report the accident to your insurance company if you do not believe you were at fault, it is important to do so anyways for a few reasons. First, it is possible that the driver who is responsible did not have any insurance at all. If this is the case, and assuming you had full coverage (collision, liability, and uninsured motorist) you will want your insurance company to evaluate your vehicle for damage as soon as possible. This means you will need to know where your vehicle was towed.

If the accident was the fault of the other driver, their insurance company may quickly notify you in an effort to obtain a quick settlement and release all liability against their insured (the driver at fault). Many times their insurance adjuster will offer a quick settlement of the property damage of the car but only if you will settle the whole claim – including any personal injuries. If you refuse to settle the whole claim, they may tell you that the process can be drawn out and tedious.

We encourage you to resist the temptation to settle your claim quickly because of fear and uncertainty. In these circumstances, you may need to obtain a rental car and settle the property damage with your own insurance company. Your insurance company will normally recover their money from the insurance company of the person who caused the accident.

Hopefully, you have coverage for a rental vehicle. Generally, you will have to use the rental vehicle until your insurance company presents you with an offer to settle your property damage. You are expected to receive the fair market value of your car at the time of the accident. The fair market value of your car is determined to be the difference between the value of the car before the accident and the value of the car after the accident.

Another reason you may want to - or have to - work with your insurance company is that the responsible party (or the insurance company) may not get back with you very quickly. The responsible party's insurance company may be very slow. It could be days or longer before an insurance adjuster gets back with you. If this is the case, you may be without transportation for quite a long time. This affects your daily life in a number of ways, as you likely will need to have transportation to work, the grocery store, pick up your children, etc. Even if you have to work with your insurance company to settle the value of your car, the responsible party's insurance company will eventually have to pay your insurance company back through a process called arbitration. Be assured that your insurance company will not likely suffer any losses as they know how to get their money back.

If you get a call from the responsible party's insurance company, they may want to take a recorded statement from you. If this is the case, you should either proceed with extreme caution or avoid doing so at all. At the time they call, you may be asleep or have taken some form of pain medication for your injuries. You may not understand all the questions being asked and how they relate to your accident. They may also offer you money to settle your case quickly. Remember, if you sign a release and accept their check for your car damage and your injuries, the claim could very well be over. It is best to avoid a recorded statement if you can and speak to a qualified attorney before you do anything. If nothing else, it will put your mind at ease.

With respect to the value of your vehicle, keep in mind that your insurance company does not have to buy you a brand new car. They only have to pay you the fair market value of the vehicle, as we previously discussed. Though you may believe that insurance companies use the Blue Book or NADA value to determine what they pay, unfortunately, this is not the case. Insurance companies use their own evaluation in determining the value of your car. If the NADA or Kelly's Blue Book value is favorable to you, it should be submitted to the adjuster. Published market reports can many times be admitted into evidence to establish value in a trial. Some insurance companies are offering new replacement value, but these are the exception, not the rule. These companies charge a higher premium on the front end to their insured to cover their risk of paying a higher claim.

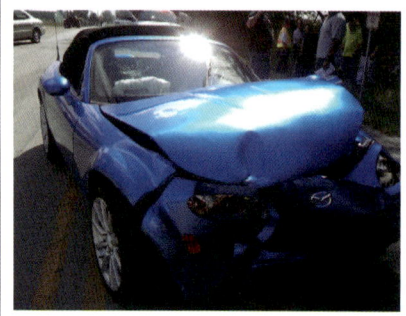
Do your research so you can get the best value and compensation for your vehicle if it was determined to be a total loss as a result of the accident.

One way to get the best value for your vehicle is to go online and find out what your vehicle would have sold for in or around the community in which you live. Many websites which deal with this issue are used to obtain a better price than that which the insurance company may offer. Put together three or four of these examples to use in dealing with the insurance company to get fair market value for the car. (For example: If you own a Honda, go to a Honda dealer's website in your county and see what a used Honda similar to yours would get in the open market.)

Finally, you may have to use your **uninsured or underinsured motorist (UIM) coverage**. This means that the other party did not have insurance - or did not have enough insurance - at the time of the collision. An example of this would be the party who only has $25,000 worth of liability insurance and you have $100,000 of uninsured/underinsured motorist (UIM) insurance. If your medical bills are $30,000, you still might be able to recover an additional sum from your UIM carrier (i.e. the difference between $100,000 and $25,000 or an additional $75,000). Your UIM carrier would pay the $5,000 difference in the medical bills. You would still have $70,000 on your uninsured motorist portion of your policy to compensate you for pain and suffering, lost wages, etc. When this issue comes up, it may be best to consult someone qualified to answer these types of questions.

A NOTE ABOUT INSURANCE COMPANIES AND SOCIAL MEDIA

Be wary of social media in the wake of your accident – Facebook, Twitter, Instagram, blogging etc. Social media can ruin your case in a heartbeat. Let us explain. You are claiming a painful injury to your neck and back after a motor vehicle accident three weeks earlier. You have told the insurance company you have been unable to leave the house, work or do chores for the last three weeks. Two days after the accident, however, you posted several photos of you and your friends fishing and swimming. There is even a picture of you lifting what looks like a portable grill while smiling into the camera.

Avoid using social media while your claim is pending.

Insurance companies are highly aware of social media. It is now one of their newest forms of surveillance in the injury business. What people do not realize is that the insurance company may be looking over your shoulder while you are not giving it a thought. If you have posted something on social media without thinking about your injury claim- think again. **It is best not to use social media at all while you are involved in a personal injury claim.**

From the Flexer Law blog:

Could Your Facebook Page Be Used Against You in a Personal Injury Lawsuit?

If you are involved in a personal injury lawsuit, even the private content of your Facebook page may be used as evidence...

In a personal injury lawsuit in Lancaster County, Pennsylvania, a judge has issued an order to hire a "neutral forensic computer expert" to review the plaintiff's Facebook account to see if there is evidence supporting her account of her injuries.

Ms. Grace Perrone claims that she slipped and fell in a puddle of liquid in an elevator at Lancaster Regional Medical Center and is suing the hospital as well as their housekeeping service for injuries she allegedly sustained to her knee and back as a result.

The judge's order grants limited discovery for a neutral third-party to review activity on Ms. Perrone's private Facebook page for the 17-day period after this alleged incident. Defense attorneys claim Ms. Perrone was photographed playing in the snow. They argued that these photographs show that she was able to engage in activities that would not have been feasible for someone with the type of injuries that Ms. Perrone claims she sustained. The defendants also claim these images show that the plaintiff had "no visible indications of pain whatsoever."

The Legal Intelligencer reports: "Information available on a person's public page, or lack thereof, has become the predominant standard among state judges in granting or denying access to a party's entire private Facebook or other social media account."

Ms. Perrone has argued that the photos and videos on her Facebook page were taken before the slip and fall incident. This means the Court will need to determine the dates on which the photos were actually taken as opposed to when they were actually posted on the social media site.

Posted on the Flexer Law blog on May 23, 2013:
http://flexerlaw.com/facebook-page-used/

SLIP AND FALL ACCIDENTS

In the introduction to this book, we discussed the slip and fall at the grocery store. If you should be unfortunate enough to experience a situation like this, there are several things you might want to do as soon as possible.

You should make sure to have a store manager fill out an incident report. All stores should have a report to fill out in the event of an accident as part of their policy or procedures. The incident report will have a place to document the store location, date and time of the accident, the injuries sustained in the accident, how the accident happened, and names of witnesses who may have seen what happened. If able, you should try to obtain a copy of this report at the earliest possible time. You should get the actual store number (i.e. Jones Grocery Store #103) and the address of the store where you fell. This way, you can send the store a letter letting them know you are making a claim for the injuries, the date the injury occurred, the person(s) you spoke with, and your claim for injuries.

The store has a legal duty to provide its customers with a reasonably safe place to shop. This would include merchandise safely placed on shelves, floors without standing liquids on them, adequate lighting, etc. The store breaches its duty when it allows a dangerous condition for shopping and you have been injured as a result.

The store has defenses such as the liquid had not been on the floor long enough for them to discover it and clean it up. As you can see, these types of cases can be won or lost on facts and details. Statements you make can be twisted, so stick to the facts and don't ramble on if you give a brief statement.

Another thing you should consider is obtaining video surveillance of the area in which you fell. Most stores these days have video evidence of aisles, entrances and the like. It is very important that any letter you send the store, or ultimately their insurance company or risk management department, include a statement asking them for a copy of the video footage. At the very least, it would be wise to ask them not to destroy any videotape evidence or surveillance they have which might show your fall or accident as it occurred. In the event they destroy the videotape surveillance after you have requested that it not be destroyed, this will not look good for the store. Many cases can be won or settled because the store erased or lost their videotape surveillance.

Most stores have video surveillance. Be sure to request a copy of the videotape or, at the very least, request that the store not destroy their video surveillance footage from the time of your accident.

Again, you may receive a telephone call from the store, its insurance company, or risk management team to give a statement with respect to how you fell. The same instructions apply as the one involving a motor vehicle accident. It might be a good idea to seek some legal counsel before giving the insurance company or the store management any information about how the accident occurred, your injuries, or otherwise. Proceed cautiously!

Finally, it would be a wise idea to check online as to the policy and procedures of a store's requirements with respect to keeping aisle ways clean, mats on floors, other safety requirements, etc. Sometimes, you can Google the name of the place in which you fell and might be able to obtain their policies and procedures with respect to store maintenance. If you are able to obtain this, be sure to make a copy of this so that you can use this in prosecuting your claim. These policies and procedures can be very beneficial to you in trying to settle your case. If a lawsuit is filed, policy and procedure manuals can be turned over if requested during the pre-trial discovery process.

DOG BITE CLAIMS

Another very common claim would be a case involving a dog bite. Needless to say, this can be a very frightening as well as painful experience. Most counties in Tennessee have some type of ordinance (law) requiring dogs to be on a leash. Our state law discusses the dog owner's responsibility if the dog is running at large (without the owner being present). [See Tennessee Code Annotated 44-8-408.] In this event, the owner may well be responsible for your injuries. This is called strict liability and the owner has few, if any, defenses available should this occur. You don't have to prove a breach of a duty, just that the event occurred (the failure to leash the dog with resulting injuries).

For Nashville and Davidson County, TN residents: Metro Davidson County Ordinance 8.01.110 discusses what is meant by a dog "running at large" and the penalties for the same.

In the event you are a victim of a dog bite, it is important that the county animal control unit be contacted immediately. This creates a record of the incident. This will document the dog's name, owner, and address of the owner, as well as what occurred. The dog may be quarantined for a time to determine whether or not it has rabies. This can be critical because if the dog is rabid, you would unfortunately have to get costly rabies shots so as to not contract this dreadful disease.

Medical treatment is critical. You will either be taken by ambulance to a nearby hospital or have someone take you for treatment. If the wounds are bad enough, surgery or stitches could be required.

Photographs of the injuries are also critical. Depending upon the location of the bites, these photos will be important in determining the value of the case. A facial bite is especially critical as it affects your overall appearance and is important not only for one's social life but for working with the general public. Facial scars can cause one great mental stress and self-consciousness. These types of injuries can cause great despair to the dog owner's insurance company because of their value.

Normally, homeowner's insurance or renter's insurance of the pet owner is the "deep pocket" out of which a settlement is paid. Regrettably, unlike auto insurance, there is no Tennessee state law requiring pet owners to have insurance. Lack of insurance can, of course, make recovery difficult but certainly not impossible. Once the court decides fault, a judgment can be issued against the responsible party.

Once someone has a judgment against them, their wages can be garnished and/or a lien can be placed on their home or other real estate they own or any money or property they may inherit from someone. Nobody wants a judgment against them or to be forced into bankruptcy (some types of accidents cannot be wiped out by bankruptcy), so most folks want to try to settle a case if they know they were at fault.

Investigating a dog bite case is very important. Animal control units in most counties in Tennessee have records reflecting previous dog bites in their particular area. Some may have records by the name of the dog. A dog who has previously bitten will most assuredly cost its owner or that insurance company damages payable to you. Make sure as part of the investigation of your case, you contact your local animal control unit to obtain a copy of the report as well as any reports of previous bites by this dog.

A final note: it is easy now these days to locate what your county or city's ordinances (laws) are with respect to animal control. Most of the time you can simply go to the county or city's website and they will have the laws posted there. If not, simply do an online search for your city or county's name along with the words "animal control law" and you can often find it there. If not, contact the animal control unit in your area, and they can direct you to the right place to obtain this information.

DEATH CLAIMS

More often than not, wrongful death claims occur as a result of a very violent motor vehicle collision. These collisions will often occur as a result of an impact with a standard motor vehicle or an over-the-road tractor trailer carrier. The motor vehicle may be mangled beyond recognition. The aftermath of these collisions is quite tragic. If a family member or loved one is unfortunately involved in such a terrible collision, you absolutely want to talk with someone who has experience handling these types of claims.

In addition, any time a death is involved, criminal charges may be filed against the driver who caused the wreck that resulted in a death. Blood alcohol levels and drug tests of the at-fault driver will need to be taken as well. If intoxication is found, another type of damages may be available. **Punitive damages** can be quite large as a jury or judge may wish to punish the wrongdoer and try to deter such behavior in the future.

Nevertheless, you will always want to obtain the motor vehicle accident report to determine what vehicles were involved and the name(s) of the driver(s). If one of the at-fault drivers was driving an 18-wheeler or over-the-road tractor trailer or interstate carrier, there are other avenues that you might want to seek in doing your research. The companies who own interstate carriers generally carry very large liability coverage insurance policies. When looking at the motor vehicle accident report, make sure you take a good look at the United States Department of Transportation identification number and record it when doing your research.

The Federal Motor Carrier Safety Administration website (https://www.fmcsa.dot.gov/) has a number of topics you can review. These topics are numerous but the major areas are as follows: regulations, registration, safety, news, and FAST Act. Once you click on the area, there are subdivisions you can review to further narrow your search. For example, if you have a question about driver safety, hit the safety link and you will see the words "driver safety" pop up. The Federal Motor Carrier Safety Administration website is very helpful with respect to regulations regarding truck drivers. It is always best to review this website when dealing with an over-the-road carrier.

When the accident is the fault of another driver, you will need to make sure to bring any claim in the name of the estate of the loved one who has passed away. If there is a will, any claim must be brought by the executor of the estate; if there is no will, it might be best to set up an estate to name an administrator. This will require going to the courthouse where the deceased lived and have the judge name an administrator. There will be filing fees involved to do this. Therefore, it is best to contact your local probate court, chancery court, or circuit court (depending on your jurisdiction) to find out how much it will cost to set up an estate. If you decide to have an attorney assist you, your attorney will generally set this up for you.

Funeral expenses are also a part of the estate's damages. It is important that you obtain the funeral bill from the funeral service in order to pursue the claim. The cost of a funeral in today's world is very expensive. Do not forget to obtain the bill as this is a very important part of the claim.

Always remember to obtain all ambulance bills, hospital bills, and emergency room physician's bills from the date of the collision until such time that your loved one passes. These bills can be quite expensive and are a major part of the claim.

There are many elements that determine the amount of financial recovery that the surviving family members may receive -- medical bills, funeral expenses, and the pecuniary (monetary) value of your loved one's life are a few elements to consider.

The **pecuniary value**, or monetary value, of your loved one's life is a very important element of the wrongful death claim. This means that if your loved one's life was cut short due to the fault of another, that person is responsible for payment to you and your family for that loss as well. Depending on the amount of the insurance coverage available, this could mean quite a large sum to be paid to the estate. Let's explain how this works.

An example would be a 40-year-old husband and father of 2 young children has been killed as a result of an accident with an over the road truck driver. The father has a job as a welder for a local construction company earning $60,000 per year. He also has health insurance benefits and is involved in a pension program. He might also have stock options with his company. This man's death will create a great financial hardship on the family. It will be necessary to have both a vocational expert and an economist to determine the value of this man's pecuniary value to the family, since he probably had another 25 years to work. Using various formulas, these experts can determine the pecuniary, or monetary, loss to the family which could stretch well into hundreds of thousands - or millions - of dollars. Again, the final settlement depends on the insurance coverage that the responsible party has available and your uninsured/underinsured insurance.

GOVERNMENTAL NEGLIGENCE

There are times when the government can be negligent. There are special rules when bringing a case against the government. If you can prove fault against the government, you can recover money damages. Cities or counties can be at fault and the state can be at fault. The important thing to remember is that a case against the government may require stricter proof.

Cases against a state government must be filed in a certain place. In Tennessee, if the claim is not filed in the Tennessee Division of Claims within a certain time period (1 year), it is very likely that you will not be able to recover for your claim. Furthermore, claims against the county or state government are not tried in front of a jury. Only a trial judge or claims commissioner can hear these cases.

Cases against the county and/or state can be much like cases against private individuals or corporations. These cases usually involve motor vehicle collisions against governmental employees. Others, however, can involve such instances as bullying of a student, falling in a school building, or a traffic control fence inexplicably falling and injuring an innocent pedestrian. Sometimes, these cases can involve death where the governmental entity fails to protect the life of a student or a prison inmate. Knowing the law and understanding the case against the government requires a great deal of time, attention and expertise.

CASES INVOLVING FEDERAL, STATE AND COUNTY GOVERNMENTS

Cases against the state and county governments are a more modern phenomenon as personal injury cases are concerned. In the early days of the United States, an individual was not able to bring a case against a governmental unit under a doctrine known as "sovereign immunity." This dates back to the days in England when a king could do no wrong. The king could not be sued during the reign of the monarch, hundreds of years ago.

Now, suits against governmental entities are allowed, provided certain requirements are met. Did you even know you could file a claim against the United States government if you have been the victim of a personal injury? An example of such a claim would be if you're rear-ended by the driver of a U.S. Postal Services truck. You are entitled to file a claim against the U.S. Government under the Federal Tort Claims Act. You must first file a claim under this act and try to resolve your claim before you are allowed to file a lawsuit. If you are unable to settle the claim with them, you are then permitted to file a claim against the United States Government in an appropriate court.

Claims against the State of Tennessee are also permitted. If you are injured due to the fault of the government or one of its employees, you will want to file a claim in the Division of Claims. This is a requirement before filing suit against the State of Tennessee. Once the Division of Claims receives your claim, they have 90 days to investigate your claim. After 90 days, they will generally send a denial letter which allows you to file suit against the State. Such a lawsuit must be filed with the Tennessee Claims Commission. A suit filed against the State of Tennessee will be tried in front of a State Commissioner who has the same authority as a judge. There are three state commissioners who hear these personal injury cases against the state government. There is a commissioner in West Tennessee, Middle Tennessee, and East Tennessee. There are no jury trials in claims against the state.

A lawsuit against the State of Tennessee is no different than a claim against a private citizen or corporation. You have one (1) year from the date of your injury to file a claim against the State of Tennessee. If you do not file your suit within that time period, you will be unable to receive compensation for your injuries.

Claims against the county are also permissible in Tennessee. In the event you are injured due to the fault of the county or a county employee, the first thing you should do is notify the Risk Management Division of the county documenting your injury due to the fault of a county employee or the county's failure to do something they should have done to prevent your injury. You should make sure you check with the local county to determine where to send a copy of your claim. The Governmental Tort Liability Act in Tennessee governs how claims are filed against local governments in this state.

Lawsuits against the county are filed in the circuit court in the county in which the incident occurred. The lawsuit against the county would be heard by a judge - once again, no juries are allowed in cases against the county (with some exceptions). Similar to lawsuits against the state, you have one (1) year to file your suit against the county in the State of Tennessee.

AFTER YOU HAVE FINISHED MEDICAL TREATMENT

You have finished receiving treatment for your injuries. You are probably wondering: "What do I do now?" This can be very stressful, especially if you have seen numerous healthcare providers. Hopefully, you have kept copies of all of your medical bills and have written down the names of all of your providers. If not, you will need to obtain the names and addresses of all providers.

You will have to sign a **HIPAA form** before you or someone else can obtain your medical bills and medical records. The purpose of the HIPAA form is to maintain your privacy and to keep your medical records confidential. This form is an authorization allowing the medical provider to turn the medical records over to you or your representative. The medical records and bills are used by the insurance company as part of the formula to determine the amount you are to be compensated.

> *HIPAA stands for the Health Insurance Portability and Accountability Act which was passed by Congress in 1996.*

There are a few things that the insurance company are especially interested in when evaluating your case. First, they want to determine if there were any broken bones. Second, they want to determine if there were any herniated discs or torn ligaments. Third, they want to determine whether or not there were any surgeries involved as a result of your injuries. They also want to know if you were scarred or disfigured in any way as a result of the accident.

What about your lost time from work? Lost wages have been discussed already as another element of your damage. You will always want to obtain a letter from your doctor outlining the amount of time you lost from work as a result of the accident. Time off due to having to go to your doctor appointments or physical therapy is reviewed, but the actual missed days from work is where the insurance company usually places the most emphasis when evaluating the claim.

A photograph is worth a thousand words. Photographs of damaged vehicles are extremely valuable in evaluating the case. Insurance companies are impressed with high impact collisions. The more damage to your vehicle, the more likely the insurance company will "believe" you were injured as a result of this accident. We know that injuries can occur when there is very little visible damage to the vehicle. Unfortunately, the insurance company will not pay very much money when they are unable to see the damage to your vehicle. Likewise, juries - especially in Middle Tennessee - are unlikely to award damages in a case involving minimal property damage.

A picture is worth a thousand words. Submitting photos of the damage to your vehicle can help the insurance company and/or the jury understand the severity of the accident.

INSURANCE RESERVES

After you have been involved in a motor vehicle accident, you will probably get a phone call from the insurance adjuster. You may want to avoid giving a recorded statement. You will probably be asked about your injuries. The reason for this generally has to do with how much the insurance company will place in "reserve" in sizing up your case. The reserve is compared to how much the insurance company has set aside based on their opinion of the value of your case. Depending on the type of injuries you have and the insurance money that is available, the reserve can be adjusted as the insurance company receives updated information about the claim. Also, it is important for you to know that adjusters can only offer you so much money before they have to go to a supervisor to get permission to offer you more than they have authority to give.

YOUR DEMAND LETTER

What do you do when you're ready to settle your claim? You'll need to put together a **demand letter** asking the insurance company for monetary damages. There is a fine art in making a demand and each person has their own style in writing this type of letter. There are a few things you should include in the letter so the insurance company will be clear as to what and why you are asking for the amount demanded. Remember, the insurance company has lots of claims, so the better your letter is with inclusion of the proper information, the sooner you may get a response. Generally speaking, it takes the insurance company 30 days to evaluate your claim so make sure you keep a calendar and contact the insurance company again if you have not heard back from them within that time period.

In making your demand, state the kind of case you have. If it is an automobile accident, tell them that; if it is a dog bite case, tell them that. You should always state the date and the location of the accident and the injuries sustained. Of course, you will want to give details of the accident, the person(s) involved, how it occurred, and if citations were given to anyone.

When you're ready to settle your claim, you need to put together a demand letter to send to the insurance company.

Outline, in chronological order, your treatment for the insurance adjuster to review. If you went to the hospital by ambulance, be sure to include this in your letter. If you went to the hospital, make sure to let them know what your complaints were and every test you were given while there. Be sure to include the instructions the hospital gave you for home care or advice to see a specialist. Also include any medications they provided you or prescriptions they instructed you to fill at your pharmacy. Make sure to state what instructions the emergency room physicians or personnel gave you with regards to your work. If you have seen other providers, use the previous guidelines given to outline their treatment in this demand letter. (See Appendix A for a sample demand letter.)

Make sure you include in your demand package the following:
>1) A demand letter
>2) Any photographs of the accident and/or the scene of the accident
>3) Any and all photographs of the injuries
>4) A specific list of all your medical providers and a list of all your medical bills, with a total of the bills
>5) A copy of all your medical bills and medical records
>6) Any citations that were given to the other responsible party/parties

A word about soft tissue injuries: Soft tissue injuries generally involve some injury to muscles, tendons and/or ligaments. When your neck is involved, injuries such as these are widely known as "whiplash injuries."

These injuries are quite painful and can have long lasting effects. Unfortunately, in this day and time, most insurance companies are not willing to pay large amounts for the typical soft tissue injury. Juries in the middle Tennessee area typically do not award large sums either. This is a fact. Nevertheless, soft tissue injuries in claims **do** have value so never sell yourself short if you have a claim such as this.

I CAN'T SETTLE MY CASE - WHAT NEXT?

You have sent your material to the insurance company but you can't seem to settle your claim - what is the next step? It looks like you are going to have to file a lawsuit against the responsible party. In doing so, you must be sure you are filing suit against all responsible parties. Let us give you an example.

You have been involved in an automobile collision with an 18-wheeler - a commercial truck. The driver of the 18-wheeler was unable to bring his/her vehicle to a stop while traveling along the interstate and hit you while you were stopped in traffic. Your vehicle was totaled and you sustained very painful injuries. Of course, you have to name the driver as a party in the lawsuit, but you must also include the owner of the 18-wheeler as he/she is what we call "the deep pocket." The owner of the 18-wheeler is an **indispensable party** and must be sued before your time limit runs out (**statute of limitations**).

> *The **statute of limitations** for personal injuries in Tennessee is one year from the date of the injury accident. If a lawsuit is not filed on or before that date, you have lost all rights to your case. There are only a few exceptions to this - so a word to the wise - <u>always</u> file your lawsuit before the one-year statute of limitation expires!*

Another good example would be the premises liability case. Suppose you slipped and fell in the ABC Department Store. Your statute of limitation runs on June 15, 2017. You file your lawsuit against the department store on June 13, 2017. You filed your lawsuit on time, right? But what if you learn on June 18th that ABC Department Store does not perform its own maintenance on the floors of the store, but rather XYZ Janitorial Service was responsible for the maintenance of the floor on which you fell? The lawsuit might fail since you did not sue the indispensable party - the XYZ Janitorial Service. There are rules that could save the case against the indispensable party but you should contact an attorney to discuss how this works.

No matter how good your case might be, if you fail to file against an indispensable party in a timely manner, your claim could be lost forever. There are exceptions to this but don't take a chance on losing your claim because of an exception. Make sure you get sound legal counseling in the event that you are unsure who you need to sue.

This can be a tricky area with complicated corporate ownership structures being as they are. It's another reason to file your lawsuit with plenty of time to discover who owns what and who is responsible for what, if it appears that a reasonable settlement with the insurance company is unlikely.

WHERE SHOULD I FILE MY LAWSUIT?

Once you have determined who to sue, your next step is to determine where to file your lawsuit. In Tennessee, you generally have to determine two things:

1) Where did the accident or injury occur? and
2) Where does the responsible party (or parties) reside?

For example, your accident occurs in Rutherford County, Tennessee (Murfreesboro, Smyrna, etc.) but the defendant lives in Dickson. You have a choice. You can file the case in Rutherford County (Murfreesboro, TN) or Dickson County (Charlotte, TN). The decision may rest on which of these two jurisdictions would be most favorable to you as a plaintiff.

The next question you must answer is: In which court should you file your case? Here again, you have two choices. Tennessee has two different courts where accident cases are usually filed. The General Sessions Court would be option one and the Circuit Court would be the other option.

Your decision is determined by the amount of monetary damages involved in your claim. The General Sessions Court in Tennessee has jurisdiction to award damages up to $24,999.00.

Also, there are no jury trials in this court. If your case involves damages greater than that amount, you must file your case in Circuit Court. Remember, cases should be filed in the court of the county where the accident (injury) occurred or where the defendant (responsible party) resides.

Most cases with damages of $10,000.00 or more should generally be filed in Circuit Court. Also, if you filed your case in Tennessee General Sessions Court but lost, you can appeal in Circuit Court and get a brand new trial.

However, keep in mind that if you file your lawsuit in General Sessions Court and you win, the party at fault can always also appeal the case. In addition, all testimony you gave in General Sessions Court under oath can be used against you in a later trial in Circuit Court.

When filing a lawsuit, remember that you are the Plaintiff and the person(s) responsible is/are the Defendant(s). If you choose to file your case in the General Sessions Court, you must file what is known as a **civil warrant**. The civil warrant must name all the parties that you intend to sue with their proper addresses and the date you wish to have your case tried in front of a judge. The warrant must include a statement as to how the accident occurred, when it occurred, and why you believe the responsible party was at fault (negligent). Also, if you wish to file your case in General Sessions Court, you will need to file a list of all your medical bills. You should also file a copy of all the actual bills themselves with the medical bill list. If your medical bills are less than $4,000, they are "presumed to be reasonable" by state law. If, however, your bills are in excess of that amount, you very likely will need to hire a medical expert to testify that the medical bills were reasonable and necessary for your treatment.

ADDITIONAL RESPONSIBLE PARTIES

Do you remember when we discussed responsible parties? Often times your lawsuit will require filing a suit against a corporation as well as a particular individual or individuals. As you may recall, these are known as "indispensable parties." If you must file a suit against a corporation doing business in Tennessee, you will need to go to the Tennessee Secretary of State's website and locate the proper agent for service of process. This is the individual or corporation assigned to accept a civil warrant or a summons for the corporation you are suing. Here is the website address:

https://tnbear.tn.gov/Ecommerce/FilingSearch.aspx

Once you get to the Secretary of State's website, go to the Business Information Search and type in the name of the business or corporation you are suing. Once you locate the proper corporation, click on the Control Number and drop down to the link that says "Registered Agent." There you will click on the link and find the name and address of the person or corporation you must sue.

After you have prepared your civil warrant, you will need to file it with the General Sessions Clerk's office. You will need to find out how much it will cost to file your warrant and bring the proper amount with you so they will accept your case. Make sure you get a receipt from the Clerk's office to prove you have paid your money. Also, do not forget to get a "stamp file" copy of your lawsuit. This is important to prove you filed your claim on time if that issue should ever come up in court. Also, this will give you the docket number of your case to which you will refer in any later filings.

Your lawsuit is filed. What happens next? Well, now you must wait to make sure that the Sheriff or a private process server (if you have hired one) has served your warrant on the at fault party/parties. This will require you to check with the General Sessions Clerk's office every couple of weeks to see if the service has been accomplished. If the Sheriff's office (or private process server) has served the named person(s) in your suit, that's great! But what if several weeks go by and your suit has not been served - or worse - it has been returned as "not found" in that county?

If the Defendant is not found, you may need to hire a private investigator to locate this individual or party. Private investigators charge a flat fee or an hourly rate. It will be necessary for them to locate the Defendant and have the lawsuit served or your case may never be heard.

>  *It is up to you to make sure your warrant is served on the at fault party/parties; until this is done, your case cannot proceed.*

You have finally gotten everyone served. Assuming the responsible party has insurance, you may get a phone call from an insurance adjuster or from an attorney representing the Defendant's insurance company. The insurance company might make an attempt to settle the case with you before turning the case over to a defense lawyer. If not, the attorney will probably need to continue the case for a period of time. The General Sessions courts tend to be very liberal about granting continuances so there would be little gain in fighting a continuance requested by the attorney. Therefore, set the case out a few weeks until a certain date and then you will know when you are ready to go to trial.

Once you have your trial date, remember to issue subpoenas to any witnesses that you think will help you in your case. If your case is one of contested liability, you will certainly want to subpoena any witness that agrees that the accident was not your fault. Be sure to have the individual's proper address so you can have them served. If you know the phone number of the individual, you will want to include that as well to make it easier for the process server. Also, do not forget to note the trial date! Your witness must know when they are to attend and, of course, the location and time.

Be aware there are fees involved in having a subpoena filed and served so make sure you contact the Clerk's office for this information before filing the subpoena. Of course, make sure your witness has been served before the trial date is scheduled.

THE TRIAL – GENERAL SESSIONS COURT

Your General Sessions trial date has finally arrived. Once you arrive at the proper location and come into the court room, it can take quite a while before your case finally comes in front of the judge. General Sessions courts are typically crowded and the dockets can be quite large especially in the larger cities. Therefore, patience is a real virtue.

Once the case is called, you will be seated at one table and your opponent(s) will be seated at another table. The judge will ask everyone to identify themselves and then ask you to give a short synopsis of what the case is about and what you expect to prove. Be sure to tell the judge the date of the incident, all the parties involved, how the incident occurred, and mention your medical bills and damages. Always make sure a judge has in front of him/her your itemized list of medical bills and the medical bills themselves.

The judge will then ask you to call your first witness. In the legal system, the Plaintiff always goes first and must prove the case by a "preponderance of the evidence." If we were to use a numbers system, this means that the court must feel like 51% of the case is more in your favor than in the Defendant's. In other words, it is more likely than not that your case has merit and you should be awarded damages. If you prove your case by a preponderance of the evidence, you should win your case.

If your medical bills are less than $4,000.00, you will more than likely not have to call any expert witness to testify. If, however, your medical bills are greater than that amount, you may have to call a witness to testify. This could be quite costly as doctors and/or chiropractors charge an expense fee just to testify in the court room.

If you must call a medical witness (only a medical doctor, osteopathic physician or chiropractor may testify) you had best line them up well before the trial date. Also, they must be able to testify that:

a) your injury was caused or aggravated by the accident,
b) your medical bills were a reasonable charge, and
c) the treatment was necessitated by the accident itself.

From a practical point of view, medical doctors will want their testimony captured at a deposition rather than attending a trial. Tennessee state law even gives medical doctors protection from having to testify live in a civil case (like an auto accident case). A typical doctor's deposition will cost between $1,500 and

$2,500 but they can cost much more with the court reporter costs.

After you have put on your proof before the court, the Defendant will have an opportunity to put on his/her proof. After each defense witness, you will have the opportunity to cross examine that individual. Cross examination is an art form. You will be asking the witness, through leading questions, a series of questions testing that individual's credibility.

An example of such an exchange is as follows:

Question: "On the date of the collision, you were operating a 2000 Ford Taurus. Correct?"
Answer: "Correct."
Question: "You own that vehicle. Correct?"
Answer: "Correct."
Question: "No one was in that vehicle with you. Correct?"
Answer: "Correct."
Question: "My vehicle was stopped at the red light at the intersection of 4th and Maple. Correct?"
Answer: "Correct."
Question: "You were unable to stop your vehicle before hitting my vehicle. Correct?"
Answer: "Correct."

In this way, you have asked a closed ended question, getting the Defendant to admit that your vehicle was stopped at a light and that he/she was the one responsible for hitting your vehicle. In this way, the Defendant is unable to give any explanation as to why your vehicle was hit.

If you prove your case by "preponderance of the evidence," which means that the court must feel like 51% of the case is more in your favor than in the Defendant's, you should win your case.

THE VERDICT

The judge has now heard all the proof and is prepared to render the verdict. The first thing the judge will have to determine is whether or not the Defendant is liable, or at fault, for the accident. In Tennessee, and in most other states, the Court will compare the fault of both parties to determine whether or not the Plaintiff has proven his or her case by preponderance of the evidence. In order to win your case, the judge must find that the Defendant is greater than 50% at fault for the accident. If the court finds both parties equally at fault - 50% to the plaintiff and 50% to the defendant - the plaintiff cannot win. This is called a defense verdict. The case will then be dismissed. If, however, the plaintiff is found to be 49% at fault and the defendant 51% at fault, then the plaintiff will win. These numbers are very important, and here's why:

Let's say you have $3,000 in medical bills and the judge finds that all medical bills were reasonable and necessary. The judge finds, however, that the Defendant was only 51% at fault. The judge then awards you $1,000 on top of the medical bills. You would receive 51% of $4,000 or $2,040 total.

This verdict would stand unless you or the defendant chooses to appeal. If there's an appeal, it must be filed within ten (10) days of the verdict, or the verdict becomes final. If an appeal is filed, it would be filed in the General Sessions Court Clerk's office and be sent to the Circuit Court Clerk, where it will eventually be given a new docket number.

THE CIRCUIT COURT CASE

Often times, cases are more complicated and involve damages greater than $25,000.00. If this is the case, you cannot file your lawsuit in General Sessions Court. You must file the case in the Circuit Court of the county in which the defendant resides or the county in which the injury occurred.

You will recall that the General Sessions case began with the filing of a civil warrant. In Circuit Court, you (the Plaintiff) will have to file a document called a **complaint**. In your complaint, you must allege the following: a short statement of the incident (accident), how it happened, the date it occurred, who was at fault, and the legal reasons why you believe the other party/parties is/are at fault. These components are called **negligence theories**. In an automobile accident, the Defendant could have been "following too closely" or "speeding" or "ran a red light." In a premises liability case, the Defendant could be "negligent" by "failing to keep the premises safe for its invitees (customers)" or "failing to warn of a wet floor."

Once you have set out the basics as to how the incident occurred, the date, time, location, and your legal theories, you must then make a claim for damages. In your Circuit Court complaint, it is generally best to list all your elements of damages. You should probably list the following:

- claim for medical expenses
- claim for pain and suffering
- claim for loss of enjoyment of life
- claim for loss of wages
- claim for loss of ability to earn income

Although you might not be able to prove an element of damage, it is always best to list every element of damage available. Better to list all elements than to leave one out.

Once you have prepared your complaint and reviewed it, it must be filed in the Circuit Court in the county where the accident occurred or where the Defendant resides. Make sure you contact the Circuit Court Clerk's office before you file the suit. Generally, you will need to have money for the Circuit Court Clerk's fee and one for the Sheriff's department if you intend to have them serve your complaint. If you do not have the Sheriff's department to serve the complaint and instead choose a private process server, you will have to pay far more than the cost of the Sherriff's fee.

You will also need to prepare what are called a **summons** and **cost bond**. The **summons** is a form which basically has a place for you to place your name as Plaintiff and the name(s) of the Defendant(s). You will more than likely have to fill out a separate summons for each Defendant. The **cost bond** is a form that you sign that basically states you will be responsible for any court cost assessed should you lose the case. (See Appendix B & C for sample forms.)

Davidson County Tennessee's Circuit Court Clerk website has a form which displays the summons with court bond:

https://circuitclerk.nashville.gov/circuit/circuitforms.asp

Checking service of process should be done every two weeks. If the Sheriff or process server makes a return "not found" you will then have to issue what is called an "alias summons." This means you must try to locate the Defendant again. Chances are, a professional private investigator will know the best way to locate the Defendant. Identifying the person by date of birth, last known address, and any other information (i.e. driver's license) will be useful in assisting the investigator.

As in the case of the General Sessions civil warrant, you might be suing a corporation. Do not forget to seek assistance at the Tennessee Secretary of State's website. Prepare your summons to include the proper name of the corporation and the name of the registered agent for service of process using, of course, the correct address. You will have your complaint attached to the summons and the cost bond when giving your documents to the Clerk.

ONCE EVERYONE IS SERVED

Once all parties have been served, you will more than likely receive a letter from a defense attorney asking you for more time to file the answer. Once again, the courts are generally very liberal about granting these continuances. Eventually, you will get the answer filed by the Defendant. When you receive the answer, take a look at your complaint and compare it side by side to the answer. You will recall that, in your complaint, you made several allegations against the Defendant. The Defendant looks at your complaint and answers each and every one of these allegations. With some exceptions, do not be surprised if the Defendant(s) deny each and every one of your allegations. This is usually a formality so do not be alarmed or upset by their denials. They are just making you work for your settlement.

Along with the answer, you will more than likely find attached a set of **discovery** requests. These usually come in the form of interrogatories and requests for production of documents. These allow the defendant to find out what your case is all about.

WHAT IS DISCOVERY?

Discovery is the way that attorneys find out information about the other side's case. Prior to the rules of discovery being adopted, attorneys would walk into a courtroom that would probably be full of surprises. When I was in law school, it was referred to as "trial by ambush" – just like the old Wild West.

The discovery rules have taken much of the guess work out of a trial. Discovery allows each side to learn what proof the other side intends to use at trial. The exchange of information, photos, documents, etc. allows us to evaluate the case and move it toward settlement. This process encourages settlement so that the courts are not as crowded.

Some of the forms of discovery include:

- **Interrogatories** are formal questions that are sent by the opposing side. Both parties have an opportunity to send out questions. These are meant to learn something about the case and the background of the person or company being sued. We have included some sample questions in this book (see pages 80-82).
- **Depositions** are a bit more like court. Even if the judge is not present, a court reporter is there and records your testimony. Depositions are not limited as to time or

number of questions asked. You are face to face with the opposing party. They are not only fact finding but designed to see how you would appear in front of a judge or jury.

- **Request for production of documents** are very important especially to a Defendant in a personal injury case. The most obvious documents the defense will want are current and past medical records. Obviously if you have a previous back condition and you are alleging a back injury, the defense will want to know about your previous complaints to other providers.
- A **request to inspect premises** is just what you think it would be. These can be especially helpful if you want to see where someone fell in a slip and fall case. If you slipped in water at a store, these can be helpful. What if the slip occurred steps from where they keep the ice? It is not a stretch to say that water could have gathered from the ice machine.
- The **request for admissions** is designed to have the other party admit to certain facts so as to limit the number of disputed facts there will be in the lawsuit.

We will go into greater detail about these types of discovery in the following pages.

INTERROGATORIES

Interrogatories are formal questions that are sent by the opposing side. Both parties have an opportunity to send out questions. These are meant to learn something about the case and the background of the person or company being sued. In some counties, there are limitations to the number of interrogatories that can be asked. In Davidson County, Tennessee, for example, you are generally limited to 30 questions.

SAMPLE QUESTIONS YOU MAY BE ASKED (INTERROGATORIES):

1. State your name, address, date of birth, and Social Security number.
2. Please state your marital status and the name(s) and age(s) of any children.
3. Please state all prior injuries that you have had in your life.
4. Please state all prior claims you have made (i.e. workers compensation claims, other personal injury claims from an accident or slip and fall, etc.)
5. State in detail the name(s) of all medical doctors you have seen in the 10 years prior to your accident.

6. Please state the name and address of all medical providers you have seen as a result of this accident.

7. Please provide a copy of all medical bills you have incurred as a result of this accident.

8. State the name(s), address(es), and telephone number(s) of any and all witnesses who saw the accident or knows about any portion of your claim including, but not limited to, your injuries, etc.

9. Please state in your own words how the accident occurred.

10. Please state whether or not you have ever been arrested or convicted; if so, please state the location of each arrest and conviction.

Similarly, the Plaintiff sends out discovery to the Defendant to learn something about this individual. Here are a few sample interrogatories to be sent to the Defendant.

INTERROGATORY SAMPLES TO SEND TO THE DEFENDANT:

1. Please state your name, address, date of birth, and Social Security number.
2. State the name and address of your current employer and the name and address of your employer at the time of the collision.
3. Provide a copy of your current driver's license (Tennessee or otherwise).
4. State the name of all owner(s) of the vehicle that was involved in the collision at the time of the collision.
5. State all lawsuits in which you have been involved, as either a Plaintiff or a Defendant, and the circumstances of each case.
6. In the 24 hours prior to the collision, state whether or not you were under the influence of any drug or alcohol and if so, state the name(s) of the drug(s) you had been taking and/or the type(s) of alcohol you had been drinking at the time.
7. State whether or not you have been arrested, pled guilty to, or been convicted of any crime. If so, state the location of the arrest, city, state, county,

8. etc. and the date of the arrest, the conviction, the crime involved, and its final resolution.

8. State whether or not you have ever had a driver's license suspended and/or revoked. If so, state the circumstances surrounding the suspension or revocation and the state in which it occurred.

9. Please state in your own words how the motor vehicle collision occurred.

10. Please state if you are making any allegations that the Plaintiff in any way caused, contributed to, or was comparatively at fault for the motor vehicle collision. If so, state in detail what the nature of your allegations will be.

Another form of discovery is a **request to inspect the premises**. Under Rule 34 of the Tennessee Rules of Civil Procedure, you can request to enter the Defendant's premises. This would be a relevant form of discovery if you fell in a store or were injured on someone's property. This is a useful tool in actually being able to inspect the site if you haven't already taken pictures.

Request for admissions is another form of discovery. Request for admissions are served upon a party in order to have the other side to admit the certain facts of to the genuineness of certain documents. Let's say you have taken photographs of the scene of an accident depicting the two damaged vehicles involved. If you want to prove that the photograph depicting the defendant's damaged vehicle is indeed seen in the photograph, a request for admissions would be appropriate. The request would be as follows: "Please admit or deny the photograph attach depicts the Defendant's vehicle immediately after the collision with the Plaintiff."

After written discovery has been sent, each side has thirty (30) days to respond with their answers to the questions (or 45 days if served with the Complaint). If no response is made at the expiration of the time limit, the Court could deem the photo or document as true.

Before the deadline passes, it is generally a good idea to send a letter to the opposing party if your answers are going to be late. Additionally, if the deadline passes and your opponent has not answered their discovery, it is a good idea to send them a letter asking them to provide you with their answers.

If the letter does not get a response within 2-3 weeks, it is a good idea to follow up with a telephone call to find out where the answers are. Document your phone call, who you spoke to, when the phone call occurred, and what was said. If, after the phone call, you get no results, you will need to file a **motion to compel discovery** in the Circuit Court Clerk's office. These motions are filed in order to receive answers to your interrogatories or questions you sent the Defendant. These motions are also filed to obtain documents you may have requested but the Defendant has not yet provided. This will usually cause the other side to respond to your request. The opposing party does not want some type of order to be signed by the judge which could ultimately result in some unfavorable sanction against their client. This would generally make an insurance company very unhappy with their attorney.

If your motion to compel is granted, you will draft an order reflecting the court's decision in how much time the Defendant is granted to comply. If the Defendant still does not comply with the Court's order, you can file a motion for sanctions. This could limit the evidence that the Defendant is able to put on at trial.

DEPOSITIONS

A deposition may be your first face-to-face encounter with the Defendant and his/her attorney. A deposition is a verbal statement under oath and everything you say will generally be taken down by a court reporter. The deposition is usually a two-hour question and answer period designed to "nail down" your testimony or what you would say if your case went to trial. It is very important that you are truthful during your deposition. Depositions test your truthfulness and your ability to answer questions in the comparatively short amount of time you are there. The more inconsistencies found in your testimony, the harder it is to win your case at trial. Also, the defense wants to see what kind of witness you will make (i.e. are you even tempered, easily angered, etc.).

A deposition may be your first face-to-face encounter with the Defendant and his/her attorney.

Generally, areas discussed in your deposition are as follows:

1) Your background (name, age, education, job experience, etc.)
2) Previous accidents and claims
3) Your past and present health
4) The accident itself
5) Your activities after the accident
6) Questions regarding your medical records and medical treatments after the accident
7) Questions about all your medical treatment prior to the accident
8) How the accident has affected your life

This, of course, is not an exhaustive list.

Costs of a deposition can vary. This usually depends on the court reporter's *per diem* fee (their charge just to be there) and how much they charge per page. A deposition can cost somewhere in the neighborhood of $300 - $500 to transcribe, again depending on the number of pages and the amount charged per page. If you wish to order the depositions of everyone deposed, you will need to make arrangements with the court reporter and find out the estimated cost. It is generally best to make arrangements the day of the deposition. You may want to get something in writing from the court reporter.

If you hire an attorney, they ordinarily will pay the deposition and court reporter costs, but will recover them out of the settlement proceeds or if you win at trial.

THE DOCTORS' DEPOSITIONS

In many cases, a doctor's deposition will not be taken before mediation in order to keep the costs of litigation down. If a doctor's deposition must be taken, the cost can be anywhere from $750 - $1,500 for the first hour of testimony. After that, doctors generally charge by the hour. When taking the doctor's deposition, it is very important to have a court reporter present to transcribe his/her testimony. Doctors are exempt from testifying live in a Tennessee court by Tennessee law. Therefore, they must always testify by deposition or by videotape deposition.

A videotape deposition requires the hiring of a videographer which can make this experience much more costly. A deposition is either shown to the jury (if by video) or read to the jury (if not videotaped). There are very strict rules about videotape depositions and it is a good idea to contact an attorney if you plan to take a doctor's deposition by videotape.

The important elements of a doctor's deposition are as follows:

- A. Qualifying the doctor as licensed in the state
- B. The history of the doctor's background, his/her education, specialty, professional associations, hospital privileges, etc.
- C. The doctor's explanation of his/her specialty and what it means to be board certified if he/she is board certified
- D. Going over all the medical notes regarding the injury

Once the doctor has done all of these things, **the doctor must be able to testify to a reasonable degree of medical certainty or probability that the accident caused or aggravated the person's injuries. The doctor must testify that the medical bills were reasonable and that they are customary charges as prescribed by other physicians in the local community. Finally, the doctor must testify that the treatment was necessitated by the auto accident or type of accident which**

you are claiming. It is always best to make the medical bills an exhibit to the doctor's deposition.

If your case requires a doctor's deposition, the doctor must be able to testify that your injuries were either caused or aggravated by the accident and that all treatment was necessary and reasonable.

MEDIATION

Just because you filed a lawsuit does not mean your case cannot be settled. Courts encourage settlement and especially encourage the parties to get into mediation. This gives both parties an opportunity to participate in the resolution of the claim.

In Tennessee, **alternative dispute resolution** has been very popular for the last 20 - 25 years. In order to become what is known as a "Rule 31 Mediator" a person must have 40 hours of training which is recognized by the Tennessee Supreme Court. It is not required that the person be a licensed attorney; however, licensed attorneys make excellent mediators in cases regarding personal injuries.

The Tennessee Administrative Office of the Court's website has a list of Rule 31 mediators. The mediator is a neutral party and does not have any stake in the claim other than to try to bring your case to successful resolution.

Most mediators in Middle Tennessee conduct mediations in the mornings and in the afternoons. As an example, a typical morning session will usually go from 9:00 AM to 12:00 PM. Sometimes, the mediation can go longer depending upon how complex your facts are. The mediations are almost always held at the mediator's office. When you arrive, you will usually be greeted by a receptionist or staff member and escorted to the mediation room. If you are represented by an attorney, your attorney will usually already be there waiting for you to discuss the case prior to the beginning of the session.

Participants in the mediation are separated into two or more rooms, depending on the number of parties. If you are represented, your attorney or representative will be in the room with you and, in another room, will be the insurance company's attorney and a representative from the insurance company (generally the adjuster). The mediator will deal with the parties <u>SEPARATELY</u>. The mediator will come into the room, introduce himself/herself, and explain the process of mediation. Generally, the mediator will state that this process will contain back-and-forth offers and counter-offers and that you do not have to settle your case at mediation if you do not want to. However, mediation is generally a very good way of trying to resolve your claim.

Never be insulted by the first offer! As one mediator I know always says, "It's not where we start, but where we end the mediation that matters." If you don't settle your claim at mediation, you have not lost anything but a little bit of time. As I have stated, most cases do settle at mediation, which proves that this process works. If a settlement is reached, the mediator will prepare a settlement document which outlines the terms of the settlement. Assuming your case is in litigation, always make sure the Defendant is responsible for the court costs. Sometimes the Defendant will pay the cost of mediation but insurance companies these days are not as willing to pay the mediation costs as they were in the "good old days."

After the settlement, the mediator will prepare a document for the court stating the case has been settled and, hopefully, you will receive your money within 30 days.

PRETRIAL MOTIONS

There are various types of pretrial motions. Two that we see most often are the motion for summary judgment and the motion *in limine.*

Simply put, a **motion for summary judgment** is similar to a motion to dismiss the case. A motion for summary judgment means that, as a matter of law, the case must be dismissed because one of the parties (usually the Plaintiff) does not have the evidence to prove the legal elements of the case. If the court dismisses the case on a summary judgment motion, the only recourse the Plaintiff would have is an appeal to the Court of Appeals. It can be quite costly to take an appeal to this court and can take several months or longer to get the case heard before them and ultimately to get a response.

The **motion *in limine*** is a motion heard generally days before the trial or on the day of the trial itself. This is a motion that is generally designed to keep evidence from being heard by the judge or in most cases by the jury. The ruling by the trial judge is important and can change the entire strategy of the parties in prosecuting their case.

EVIDENCE IN TENNESSEE: BASIC RULES

The rules of evidence in Tennessee are a broad and complex subject, but we want to examine some basic rules which will give you an idea of how things work.

The rules of evidence determine what a judge or jury gets to hear in reaching their decisions about who is at fault, to what extent, <u>and</u> how much damages should be awarded to one or more persons.

Relevance

The most fundamental rule of evidence is the rule of relevance. To be admitted, evidence must be relevant to an issue at hand. Relevant evidence must have a logical connection to the legal claim you are trying to prove or dispute. Evidence to be relevant must tend to make a fact more or less likely.

An example of relevance would be the negligent defendant who did not have a driver's license (even though he caused the collision). The fact that he/she did not have a diver's license is not relevant to the issue of his/her negligence in causing the accident.

The rules of evidence in Tennessee are a broad and complex subject; they determine what a judge or jury gets to hear in reaching their decisions about who is at fault, to what extent, <u>and</u> how much damages should be awarded.

Judges have a great deal of leeway in deciding whether evidence is relevant or not. Sometimes it can be a close judgment call. If you believe evidence is not sufficiently relevant to the issue at trial, you must stand up and object to any question that calls for an answer that is not relevant to the case.

One major exception to the rule requiring evidence to be relevant is that some evidence can be relevant, but it creates such an emotional response in the judge or jury that it would be unfair to allow the introduction of such evidence. A judge can exclude relevant evidence because it is too prejudicial.

The Rule Excluding Opinions

The rule against opinion testimony says witnesses should testify to specific facts which they personally observe, not give their opinions of what they think or who should win. The legal and factual conclusions are for the judge or jury to decide based on the facts admitted into evidence.

A major exception to the rule against opinions is the testimony of an **expert witness**. Expert witnesses are able to state opinions without personal knowledge while also reaching legal conclusions. Expert witnesses may include doctors, economists, psychologists, etc.

In order for an expert to be qualified to testify, the party must ask a series of questions about his/her qualifications before they can be accepted as an expert.

Rule Probability: Character Evidence

As a general rule, evidence of the character if a witness is not allowed to prove that the witness acted a particular way in a specific situation. The law recognizes that people don't always behave like their normal character traits. There are some exceptions under Tennessee law for allowing character evidence with certain sexual assault circumstances.

The Rule Against Hearsay Evidence

The American system of justice and due process believes it is unfair to allow into evidence verbal statements or writings from witnesses who are not present in Court. If such witnesses are not at the trial, they are not able to be cross examined. Therefore, such evidence should not be allowed.

An example of hearsay is when a witness states what someone else said. For example, it could be a witness saying, "Officer Smith said that it was the defendant's fault." Since Officer Smith is not subject to cross examination or is an "out of court declarant," that statement by the witness is excluded.

The hearsay rule, however, has many exceptions. Some exceptions are statements made about an observation right as it is happening, a **present sense impression**.

Another exception is a statement in which a witness describes their emotions, their intent, or their plans at the point in time about which they are describing. This is called a **state of mind declaration**.

Other exceptions to the hearsay rule include:

1. Excited utterances – A statement made about an event while the person speaking is under the duress of the event.

2. Records of regularly conducted activity – Business records kept in the ordinary course of business are the most common example.

3. Public records and reports – These records will need an evidentiary foundation from the office with a duty to report the public record or report.

4. Vital statistics – Birth, death, and marriage records.

5. Market reports – Such as commercial publications relied upon by persona or public in occupations.

6. <u>Reputation</u> as to character among associates or community.

This is just a small sample of the many exceptions to the hearsay rule, a rule that practically swallows itself with exceptions.

Evidentiary Foundations

In order to introduce evidence into the court record and for it to be admissible, most evidence must have a proper foundation. Different types of evidence require different foundations.

A **foundation** includes a witness's competence to testify, and an exhibit's relevance, identification, and trustworthiness or authentication.

An exhibit must also comply with the hearsay rule and rules regarding original documents. Foundations are commonly necessary for business records, photographs and videos, diagrams, and prior inconsistent statements, just to name a few.

Statements to a Medical Professional

Another important exception to the hearsay rule is a statement to a medical professional (doctor, nurse, etc.) for purposes of treatment or diagnosis. The statement normally must relate specifically to the treatment or diagnosis by the medical professional, not everything said during the conversation.

The reason behind all three exceptions to the hearsay rule is that there are certain types of statements that are normally sufficiently reliable and they help the judge or jury reach a reasonable verdict such that evidence should be allowed.

There are other exceptions to the hearsay rule too numerous to mention here, but the guiding principle is whether you can convince the judge that the hearsay is nonetheless trustworthy and should be admitted.

We have barely scratched the surface on the rules of evidence, but we hope you have a better understanding that the rules are to encourage reliable evidence for a judge or jury to consider in reaching their verdict. Keep this in mind and any arguments as to why evidence should be admitted or excluded will have a better chance of a favorable ruling. Emphasize why evidence is reliable or why it is unreliable when attempting to persuade the judge to rule for you.

Also, keep calm. Even excellent lawyers can get tied up in knots with certain evidence issues. Most trials are not won or lost on the admission or exclusion of a piece of evidence, although they certainly can be,

Judges encourage and sometimes insist on detailed stipulations (agreements between the two sides as to the facts that are not in dispute) which act as evidence. This streamlines trials and keeps them moving.

Motions in limine resolve evidence issues before the trial. Nonetheless, despite stipulations and *motions in limine* ,trials are fluid, think-on-your-feet experiences. Wise use of objections when necessary can be a potent weapon in litigation. However, when used unnecessarily, objections are extremely irritating to a judge or jury and can make the lawyer or Plaintiff look extremely silly.

Don't object just because you can. Decide whether the evidence really hurts your case, but be decisive if you decide to object. Most judges and juries don't really like lawyers who try to show off how smart they are if the evidence in question is not very important. Finally, tend to err on the side of caution.

THE TRIAL – CIRCUIT COURT

The day of your personal injury trial has finally arrived. Of course, you want to make sure that you are dressed appropriately. Remember, a judge or jury will be sitting in judgment of you and your appearance is quite important. You do not have to wear a sport coat or suit or your Sunday best dress. You should look neat and be dressed nicely and you will be just fine.

The first order of business will be picking a jury if this is a jury trial. If it's a bench trial, then you will be giving opening statements. In most cases, a jury trial is 12 persons, but in a civil matter such as this, it is not unheard of to have a 6-person jury. Six person juries are usually by request of the plaintiff, but the defendant can turn around and ask for a 12-person jury. Assuming this is a jury trial, you will have an opportunity to "*voir dire*" the jury. **Voir dire** in French means "to speak the truth." This allows the parties to find out something about the potential jurors and allows you to determine whether or not you want this person to sit on your jury. You and your attorney or representative (should you have one) will have the opportunity to ask potential jurors questions after the judge has asked a series of preliminary questions.

You have the opportunity to dismiss potential jurors. For example, a "challenge for cause" can be requested if a juror has a specific bias against individuals who bring lawsuits or people who are injured. The other type of challenge is a "preemptory challenge." This challenge can be used if you have the feeling that this prospective juror might not be favorable to your case. You do not need to have a specific purpose to dismiss this person. They can be dismissed just simply because you don't have a good feeling about them. You are limited to the number of preemptory challenges you have. You are not limited to the number of challenges for cause that you may have.

After a jury has been selected, each side has a chance to give an opening statement. The opening statement gives the jury an idea of what your case is about and what you intend to prove. A clear and well put together opening statement will go a long way toward getting jurors to start believing that yours is the more favorable position. Some have even said that cases are won or lost after the opening statements. Keep in mind that jurors must hear all the evidence before they make a decision.

You must stick to your theory of the case and not use the opening as an opportunity to attack your opponent or the jury system. Tell the jury what you <u>will</u> prove and then prove it. If you exaggerate and promise to prove things you wind up not proving, you will destroy your credibility. Make it interesting – but be very careful what you promise. Jurors will hold you to your promises.

Just as we discussed in the General Sessions case, in Circuit Court the Plaintiff puts on their proof first. In addition to any live witnesses you will call, remember that you must read the doctor's deposition to the jury if it was not videotaped. As we said earlier, the doctor's deposition is critical because you have to prove that your injuries were caused or aggravated by the accident and your medical bills were reasonable and necessary. The Defendant puts on its proof after you have called your final witness. Once all witnesses for you have testified and have been cross examined, you will rest your case.

Normally, the defense attorney will make a motion that the case be dismissed because you did not meet your burden of proof. You may also ask for a directed verdict that requests a verdict in your favor because the defense did not establish any reasonable defense to your case. If either of these motions is granted, there is no longer any need for the case to go to a jury. These motions are normally not granted, but they certainly can be if proper proof is not entered into evidence.

Just before the final arguments, the judge will have a meeting with you and/or your attorney to tell you what he/she is going to "charge" the jury. The **jury charge** instructs the jury as to what the law is regarding your particular case. If your case involves a premises liability matter, the judge will instruct the jury as to what the law is with respect to the duties owed to a person who has an accident on an owner's premises. Since damages are involved, the court will instruct the jury of the law of damages, i.e. the right to reasonable and necessary medical expenses/reimbursement, loss of earnings, etc. The court will also instruct them as to such notions of credibility of witnesses, expert witnesses (doctors), etc.

After the charge has been given, both sides will then give their final arguments. Obviously, the final argument must try to connect all the evidence together so as to let the jury know why they should find the other party responsible and why you should be awarded damages.

The judge will then give the jury a **verdict form**. The verdict form is filled out by the jury which describes the jury's findings and what, if any, award will be given to the Plaintiff.

A sample verdict form is as follows:

1) Does the jury find that the Defendant is negligent?
   ☐ Yes ☐ No
2) Does the jury find the Plaintiff is negligent?
   ☐ Yes ☐ No
3) If the jury finds the Plaintiff was negligent, please state the percentage of negligence that should be attributed to each party.
   _____% Plaintiff
   _____% Defendant

   -- If you find the Plaintiff is more than 50% negligent, please stop here. If not, please continue. --

4) Does the jury find the Defendant caused or aggravated a preexisting condition?
   ☐ Yes   ☐ No

   -- If no, please stop here. If yes, please continue. --

5) State the amount of monetary damages to be awarded for each of the following:

$ _____ Medical bills
$ _____ Loss of earnings
$ _____ Loss of earning capacity
$ _____ Pain and suffering
$ _____ Loss of enjoyment of life

$ _____ TOTAL

_____

Signature of Jury Foreperson

After the jury has rendered their verdict, they will notify the court officer, and the court will order everyone back into the court room and the foreman will then read the verdict. Once the verdict is read, the court will ask the parties if they wish to poll the jury. This is meant for each side to make sure that the jury's verdict is unanimous. If the jury is polled and the verdict is unanimous, the jury will then be excused and the trial has come to an end.

POST TRIAL MOTION AND APPEALS

If the jury finds for the Defendant (you were more than 50% responsible for the accident), the case comes to an end. That does not mean that the case is totally over. There are motions that can be filed. Once the court enters its order, you have 30 days to file a motion for a new trial. Chances of the judge awarding you a new trial are not very good. Courts generally do not like to overturn a jury's verdict unless there is a legal issue requiring the judge to set aside the jury's verdict. If the judge denies your motion, you then have 30 days from the entry of the order to file a notice of appeal to the Tennessee Court of Appeals. The notice of appeal must be filed with the Circuit Court Clerk.

The appellate process is long, tedious, expensive and generally not successful. There must be a very good legal basis for a court to overturn a jury's verdict. Jury misconduct, incorrect court rulings on evidentiary motions, or failure to give or not give jury instruction are just a few of the grounds one can cite in asking the Court of Appeals for relief. There are very strict procedural issues with filing an appeal and the parties must file briefs with the court before arguing the case to a three judge panel. It could take a year to get your case heard and you must be patient. The court will make a written finding, usually months after you have argued your case.

Odds are highly likely if you win a large money judgment, the insurance company will file an appeal. The large costs of funding a defense of an appeal by the insurance company tends to encourage settlement. You are waiting for money you were awarded, but if the insurance company is successful on appeal, you are many times starting your case all over again. All those costs are cutting into any settlement or award you finally receive.

Your last resort is to the Tennessee Supreme Court and they do not have to automatically take your case. If they do not grant your request, your case, for all practical purposes, is over.

SUBROGRATION AND SETTLEMENT

You will recall when we discussed medical expenses that we mentioned medical pay and health insurance. If you have either or both, and if all or most of your bills have been paid by some form of insurance, the insurance companies will want some or all of their money back. Of course, if you do not receive an award, you will not be obligated to repay the insurance carrier because the judge or jury did not find your claim to be related to the accident.

If you are obligated to pay back a medical provider or health insurance company out of your settlement proceeds, some providers may give you a discount. If, for example, you owe your health insurance company $5,000, you might be able to get as much as one-third off the amount you owe. Your attorney will usually negotiate on your behalf a reduction of the amount of the lien with your insurance company.

When a case is settled, your settlement check with a court order and release will be sent to you or your attorney (if represented). The release is a document prepared by the insurance company's attorney which recites the terms of the agreement or judgment of the court. The release, simply put, is a document which states that you will no longer file any claims or lawsuits with respect to the claim related to this accident you have just resolved. Once you have signed the release document, you will receive your portion of the proceeds within 30 days. If there is an attorney involved, your portion will be reduced by attorney's fees (generally 33%-40% of the total judgment or settlement, depending on whether or not the case is tried or settled without trial) and any expenses that were incurred by the attorney or the firm that represented you.

Sometimes settlements are confidential and if you ever publicly discuss the case, you could be sued by the insurance company to pay them back the settlement amount.

CONCLUSION

This book was designed to help you weave your way through the complex system involving personal injury law. The system can be frustrating and can try your patience. Hopefully you have a better understanding of what a personal injury case is like from start to finish. In the meantime, be careful on the roads, in the stores, and all along the way. The best of luck to you!

APPENDIX A: SAMPLE DEMAND LETTER

Dear Adjuster:

This is to advise you that our office represents John Smith who was involved in a motor vehicle accident with your insured on June 15, 2016 in Nashville, Davidson County, Tennessee. Specifically, our client was operating a 2010 Dodge eastbound on West End Avenue near the intersection of 21st Avenue North. Our client stopped at the red light and your insured, suddenly and without warning, slammed into the back of his vehicle, totaling the vehicle. The impact was so violent; it broke out the rear windshield of our client's vehicle. Your insured was cited for following too closely and inattentive behavior. We are enclosing photographs of both vehicles for your inspection. We have photographs of your insured's vehicle, and it appears that vehicle was totaled as well.

Mr. Smith was taken by ambulance to St. Thomas Midtown Hospital. At that time, he complained to medical personnel of pain in his neck, shoulder, and low back. He was provided X-rays and there appeared to be no fractures. He was given a neck brace and was prescribed pain medications and muscle relaxers to be taken as needed. It was recommended by the medical personnel that he stay off work for three (3) days. Finally, an orthopedic referral was made while he was at the hospital.

On June 18, 2016, Mr. Smith presented to Dr. William Jones, a local orthopedic physician. Dr. Jones was given a history by Mr. Smith of the motor vehicle collision of June 15, 2016. Dr. Jones performed a physical examination and noticed muscle spasms in the cervical spine (the neck) and lumbar region (the back). He also observed that Mr. Smith had diminished range of motion in all areas of the spine. It was the doctor's recommendation that Mr. Smith attend physical therapy for 60 days and return to his office after that time.

On August 21, 2016, Mr. Smith returned to Dr. Jones after attending 24 physical therapy sessions. He was reported as having improved and Dr. Jones noted improved range of motion and felt no muscle spasms at that time. It was recommended that Mr. Smith attend more sessions of physical therapy and return to the office in 30 days.

Mr. Smith returned to Dr. Jones on September 25, 2016. At that time, his range of motion was back to normal as he was no longer having pain or discomfort.

Mr. Smith has incurred $15,610.00 in medical expenses and lost time from work in the amount of $520.00. During his recovery time, he had difficulty with shaving and showering and doing everyday tasks that he normally had no trouble with. He was unable to play ball with his 6-year-old son. He was also unable to go hiking and biking with his wife. He had a decreased range of motion in his neck and back for three (3) months, caused by the negligence of your insured. Therefore, we demand the sum of $40,000.00 to settle this claim.

Sincerely,

John Smith (or Attorney Name)

APPENDIX B: GENERAL SESSIONS WARRANT – SAMPLE
(PAGE 1)

Source: https://circuitclerk.nashville.gov/sessions/forms/formses_civil5d.pdf

APPENDIX B: GENERAL SESSIONS WARRANT – SAMPLE
(PAGE 2)

AFFIDAVIT

To the best of my information and belief, after investigation of Defendant's employment, I hereby make affidavit that the Defendant is/is not a member of a military service.

_____
Plaintiff or Attorney for Plaintiff

_____   _____
Notary Public   My Commission Expires

ORDER

Entered: _____ 20____   _____, Metropolitan General Sessions Court
                              Judge, Division

ORDER

Entered: _____ 20____   _____, Metropolitan General Sessions Court
                              Judge, Division

ORDER

Entered: _____ 20____   _____, Metropolitan General Sessions Court
                              Judge, Division

NOTICE

TO THE DEFENDANT(S):

Failure to appear and answer this Summons will result in judgment by default being rendered against you for the relief requested. Tennessee law provides a ten thousand dollar ($10,000) personal property exemption from execution or seizure to satisfy a judgment. If a judgment should be entered against you in this action and you wish to claim property as exempt, you must file a written list, under oath, of the items you wish to claim as exempt with the clerk of the court. This list may be filed at any time and may be changed by you thereafter as necessary; however, unless it is filed before the judgment becomes final, it will not be effective as to any execution or garnishment issued prior to the filing of the list. Certain items are automatically exempt by law and do not need to be listed; these items include items of necessary wearing apparel (clothing) for yourself and your family and trunks and other receptacles necessary to contain such apparel, family portraits, the family Bible, and school books. Should any of these items be seized, you would have the right to recover them. If you do not understand your exemption right or how to execute it, you may wish to seek the counsel of a lawyer.

Source: https://circuitclerk.nashville.gov/sessions/forms/formses_civil5d.pdf

APPENDIX C: CIRCUIT COURT SUMMONS – SAMPLE

CIRCUIT COURT SUMMONS	NASHVILLE, TENNESSEE

STATE OF TENNESSEE
DAVIDSON COUNTY
20TH JUDICIAL DISTRICT

☐ First
☐ Alias
☐ Pluries

_____
_____
_____ Plaintiff

Vs.

_____
_____
_____ Defendant

CIVIL ACTION
DOCKET NO. _____

Method of Service:
☐ Davidson County Sheriff
☐ Out of County Sheriff
☐ Secretary of State
☐ Certified Mail
☐ Personal Service
☐ Commissioner of Insurance

To the above named Defendant:

You are summoned to appear and defend a civil action filed against you in the Circuit Court, 1 Public Square, Room 302, P.O. Box 196303, Nashville, TN 37219-6303, and your defense must be made within thirty (30) days from the date this summons is served upon you. You are further directed to file your defense with the Clerk of the Court and send a copy to the Plaintiff's attorney at the address listed below.

In case of your failure to defend this action by the above date, judgment by default will be rendered against you for the relief demanded in the complaint.

ISSUED: _____

RICHARD R. ROOKER
Circuit Court Clerk
Davidson County, Tennessee

By: _____
Deputy Clerk

ATTORNEY FOR PLAINTIFF	
or	
PLAINTIFF'S ADDRESS	Address

TO THE SHERIFF:

Please execute this summons and make your return hereon as provided by law.

RICHARD R. ROOKER
Circuit Court Clerk

Received this summons for service this _____ day of _____, 20____.

_____
SHERIFF

♿ To request an ADA accommodation, please contact Dart Gore at (615) 880-3309.

Source: https://circuitclerk.nashville.gov/circuit/forms/formcir_summonscivil.pdf

APPENDIX D: CIRCUIT COURT COST BOND - SAMPLE

IN THE CIRCUIT COURT OF DAVIDSON COUNTY, TENNESSEE
TWENTIETH JUDICIAL DISTRICT, STATE OF TENNESSEE

_____ }
Plaintiff(s)   }
                               }
              vs.   }   Docket No. _____
                               }
_____ }
Defendant(s)   }

COST BOND

I/We, _____

as Principal(s), and _____
as Surety, are held and firmly bound unto the Circuit Court Clerk of Davidson County, Tennessee, for the payment of all costs

The Principal(s) is/are commencing legal proceedings in the Circuit Court for the Twentieth Judicial District, at Nashville, Tennessee. If the Principal(s) shall pay all costs which are adjudged against them, then this obligation is void. If the Principal(s) fail(s) to pay, then the Surety shall undertake to pay all costs adjudged against the Principal(s). Mandated at T.C.A. §20-12-120, et seq.

PRINCIPAL(S):

PRINCIPAL	PRINCIPAL
Address	Address
Employer	Employer
Employer's Address	Employer's Address
Principal (signature), or by	Principal (signature), or by
Principal Attorney (signature)	Principal Attorney (signature)

SURETY

_____
(Print or Type Surety)

BPR # _____

_____   _____
SIGNATURE OF SURETY   ADDRESS

[Rev. 7-1-07]

Source: https://circuitclerk.nashville.gov/circuit/forms/formcir_costbond.pdf

APPENDIX E: CIRCUIT COURT SUBPOENA – SAMPLE
(PAGE 1)

STATE OF TENNESSEE DAVIDSON COUNTY Circuit Court	**SUBPOENA** ☐ TESTIMONY/PRODUCTION REQUIRED **(SEE NOTICE BELOW)** ☐ MEDICAL RECORDS **(SEE HIPAA REQUIREMENT BELOW)**	CIVIL ACTION DOCKET NO. _____
PLAINTIFF	DEFENDANT vs.	

TO: (NAME, ADDRESS & TELEPHONE NUMBER OF WITNESS)

Method of Service:
☐ Davidson County Sheriff
☐ Personal Service
☐ Out of County Sheriff

You are hereby commanded to appear at the time, date and place specified for the purpose of giving testimony. In addition, if indicated, you are to bring the items listed. Failure to appear may result in contempt of Court which could result in punishment by fine and/or imprisonment as provided by law.

TIME	DATE	ITEMS TO BRING:
PLACE	Circuit Court Clerk 1 Public Square, Room 302 Nashville, TN 37201 (OR)	

This subpoena is being issued on behalf of
☐ PLAINTIFF   ☐ DEFENDANT

Attorney: (NAME, ADDRESS & TELEPHONE NUMBER)

☐ Additional List Attached
DATE ISSUED:

RICHARD R. ROOKER
Circuit Court Clerk

BY: _____
DEPUTY CLERK

ATTORNEY'S SIGNATURE:
DESIGNEE:

♿ To request an ADA accommodation, please contact Dart Gore at 880-3309.

DESIGNEE'S SIGNATURE:

☐ Testimony/Production required.

TESTIMONY/PRODUCTION NOTICE

The failure to serve an objection to this Subpoena within twenty-one (21) days after the day of service of the Subpoena waives all objections to the Subpoena, except the right to seek the reasonable costs for producing books, papers, documents, electronically stored information, or tangible things.

☐ Medical Records Requested – HIPAA notice required.

HIPAA NOTICE

A copy of this Subpoena has been provided to counsel for the patient or the patient by mail or facsimile on the _____ day of _____, 20__, so as to allow him/her twenty-one (21) days to:

(A) Serve the recipient of the Subpoena by facsimile with a written objection to the Subpoena, with a copy of the Notice by facsimile to the party that served the Subpoena, and

(B) Simultaneously file and serve a Motion for a Protective Order consistent with the requirements of T.R.C.P. 26.03, 26.07 and Local Rule §22.10.

If no objection is made within twenty-one (21) days of the above date, you shall process this Subpoena and produce the documents by the date and time specified in the Subpoena. The signature of counsel or party on the Subpoena is certification that the above Notice was provided to the patient.

SUBMIT: Original, Witness Copy & File Copy

[Revised 7/23/13]

APPENDIX E: CIRCUIT COURT SUBPOENA – SAMPLE
(PAGE 2)

RETURN ON SERVICE	
Check one: (*1* or *2* are for the return of an authorized officer or attorney; an attorney's return must be sworn to; *3* is for the witness who will acknowledge service and requires the witness' signature.)	
1. ☐ I certify that on the date indicated below, I served a copy of this Subpoena on the witness stated above by:	
2. ☐ I failed to serve a copy of this Subpoena on the witness because:	
3. ☐ I acknowledge being served with this Subpoena on the following date:	
Sworn to and subscribed before me, this _____ day of _____, 20____.	DATE OF SERVICE:
Signature of: ☐ Notary Public or ☐ Deputy Clerk My Commission Expires:	SIGNATURE OF WITNESS, OFFICER, ATTORNEY OR ATTORNEY'S DESIGNEE:

Source: https://circuitclerk.nashville.gov/circuit/forms/formcir_subpoena.pdf

APPENDIX F: GENERAL SESSIONS SUBPOENA – SAMPLE
(PAGE 1)

_____ Court _____ County Tennessee	**SUBPOENA**	Case Number
[Plaintiff's Name]	vs.	[Defendant's Name]

To: _____
[name, address, and telephone number of person to whom subpoena is directed]

Under penalty prescribed by law, you are commanded:

☐ 1. *Subpoena for Attendance at Hearing or Trial* – to appear personally before the _____ Court of _____ County, _____ [street address] _____, _____ [city/town] _____, Tennessee, on _____ [date] _____ at _____ [time] _____ a.m./p.m., and give testimony, pursuant to Rule 45.01 and 45.05 of the Tennessee Rules of Civil Procedure; when you arrive, you must remain at the court until the judge or a court officer allows you to leave;

☐ 2. *Subpoena for Production of Documentary Evidence (Books, Papers, Documents, etc.)* – to produce and permit inspection, copying, testing, or sampling of the following designated books, papers, documents, electronically stored information, or tangible things: _____
_____ and to swear or affirm that the things produced are authentic to the best of your knowledge, information, and belief, and to state whether all responsive things have been produced, pursuant to Rule 45.02 of the Tennessee Rules of Civil Procedure; the subpoenaed items must be produced at _____ [address where subpoenaed items must be produced] _____ on or before _____ [date] _____ at _____ [time] _____ a.m./p.m.;

☐ 3. *Subpoena for Inspection of Premises* – to permit inspection of the following premises: _____ [address of premises to be inspected] _____ on _____ [date] _____ at _____ [time] _____ a.m./p.m., pursuant to Rule 45.02 of the Tennessee Rules of Civil Procedure; and/or

☐ 4. *Subpoena for Deposition Testimony* – to appear personally at _____ [address of deposition location] _____ in _____ [city/town] _____, Tennessee, on _____ [date] _____, at _____ [time] _____ a.m./p.m., then and there to testify by deposition in this matter, and to bring the following items: _____
_____, pursuant to Rule 45.04 of the Tennessee Rules of Civil Procedure.

Notice for a subpoena for production of documentary evidence (#2 above) or for a subpoena for deposition testimony (#4 above): The failure to serve an objection to this subpoena within twenty-one days after the day of service of the subpoena waives all objections to the subpoena, except the right to seek the reasonable cost for producing books, papers, documents, electronically stored information, or tangible things.

This subpoena is issued on behalf of Plaintiff ☐ or Defendant ☐. The name, address, and telephone number of the issuing party's attorney are: _____.

Signature of issuing party's attorney: _____

Date Issued: _____
                                             Signature of Clerk/Deputy Clerk

                                             For Americans With Disabilities Act (ADA) assistance only, call: _____ [name & telephone number] _____.

NOTICE: YOU CAN BE FOUND IN CONTEMPT OF COURT FOR FAILING TO COMPLY WITH THIS SUBPOENA AND IF FOUND GUILTY OF CONTEMPT YOU MAY BE FINED, IMPRISONED, OR BOTH.

(This is a general form subpoena. The party issuing the subpoena is responsible for complying with any provision of law imposing additional notice requirements that apply to the pending case or to the type of records being sought under this subpoena.)

APPENDIX F: GENERAL SESSIONS SUBPOENA – SAMPLE
(PAGE 2)

_____ Court _____ County Tennessee	**SUBPOENA**	Case Number
[Plaintiff's Name]	vs.	[Defendant's Name]

RETURN OF SERVICE

Check one of the following boxes: Box 1 or Box 2 is only for the return by an authorized officer, by an attorney, or by an attorney's agent; pursuant to Tenn. Code Ann. § 23-2-105, the return by an attorney or the attorney's agent must be sworn to. Box 3 is only for the person named in the subpoena (or the authorized representative of an organization named in the subpoena) who acknowledges service, and such person must sign in the signature box below.

❑ 1. I certify that on the date indicated below I served a copy of this subpoena on (state the identity of the person served, and the place and manner of service): _____

❑ 2. I was unable to serve a copy of this subpoena on the person named in the subpoena because _____

❑ 3. I acknowledge being served with this subpoena on the date indicated below.

FOR RETURN BY ATTORNEY OR ATTORNEY'S AGENT: Sworn to and subscribed before me on this ____ day of _____, 20 ___. ❑ Notary Public or ❑ Deputy Clerk: My Commission Expires:	DATE OF SERVICE: SIGNATURE OF OFFICER, ATTORNEY OR ATTORNEY'S AGENT, OR PERSON ACKNOWLEDGING SERVICE:

(This is a general form subpoena. The party issuing the subpoena is responsible for complying with any provision of law imposing additional notice requirements that apply to the pending case or to the type of records being sought under this subpoena.)

Source: http://www.tsc.state.tn.us/sites/default/files/docs/subpoena_revised_04-12-2016.pdf

APPENDIX G: JURY VERDICT FORM - SAMPLE

1) Does the jury find that the Defendant is negligent? ☐ Yes ☐ No
2) Does the jury find the Plaintiff is negligent? ☐ Yes ☐ No
3) If the jury finds the Plaintiff was negligent, please state the percentage of negligence that should be attributed to each party.

   _____ % Plaintiff
   _____ % Defendant

-- If you find the Plaintiff is more than 50% negligent, please stop here. If not, please continue. --

4) Does the jury find the Defendant caused or aggravated a preexisting condition? ☐ Yes ☐ No

-- If no, please stop here. If yes, please continue. --

5) State the amount of monetary damages to be awarded for each of the following:

   $ _____ Medical bills
   $ _____ Loss of earnings
   $ _____ Loss of earning capacity
   $ _____ Pain and suffering
   $ _____ Loss of enjoyment of life

   _____

   $ _____ TOTAL

   _____
   Signature of Jury Foreman

INDEX

capacity to earn, 6, 14, 15, 19, 109

compensatory damages, 18

demand letter, 53-55, 115, 116

deposition, 68, 79, 87-91, 106

discovery, 30, 78-80, 82, 84-86

dog bite, 8, 36-39, 53

evidence, 25, 30, 33, 67, 68, 71, 72, 86, 95-103, 105-107

government, 45-48

HIPAA, 49

indispensable party, 57, 58, 63

insurance companies, 9, 10, 19, 21-29, 32-34, 37, 38, 49-55, 57, 59, 65, 86, 93, 94, 111-113

liability, 8, 21-23, 36, 41, 48, 58, 65, 74, 107

lien, 10, 13, 38, 112

loss of consortium, 19, 20

lost wages, 6, 14, 15, 27, 50, 75

medical bills, 9, 10, 12, 14, 18, 27, 43, 49, 55, 62, 67, 68, 72, 75, 80-82, 88, 90, 91, 106, 107, 109, 112, 117

medical pay, 9, 10, 112

motion *in limine,* 95, 103

nominal damages, 17, 18

pain and suffering, 7, 15, 17, 19, 27, 75, 109

pecuniary value, 43, 44

punitive damages, 19, 40

recorded statements, 24, 25, 52

responsible party (parties), 24, 36, 38, 43, 44, 55, 57-63, 65, 70, 107

statute of limitations, 57, 58

subpoena, 65-66, 122-125

summary judgment, 95

trial, 25, 35, 45, 47, 61, 65-68, 79, 86, 87, 89, 95, 97, 99, 103, 104, 110, 113

uninsured/underinsured motorist insurance (UIM), 22, 26, 27, 44

wrongful death, 7, 8, 19, 20, 40-45

ABOUT THE AUTHORS

Steve Karr has litigated thousands of personal injury cases over the past 30 years in Middle Tennessee and previously in Maryland and Washington, D.C. He is able to maximize settlements and jury awards for his clients with his skills of negotiation and arbitration.

Steve graduated from Vanderbilt University with a Bachelor of Arts and subsequently graduated from Nashville School of Law in 1980. He has been representing personal injury victims for over 35 years in Tennessee as well as in the Washington, D.C. area. In his spare time, Steve is an avid reader.

ABOUT THE AUTHORS

James Flexer is a Nashville native who graduated from Montgomery Bell Academy in 1974, Rhodes College in 1978, and Tulane School of Law in 1981.

In 1981, he founded his own firm, Flexer Law. He and his team of attorneys assist clients with everyday legal issues such as personal injury claims, Social Security Disability appeals, worker's compensation claims, Chapter 7 and Chapter 13 bankruptcy, divorce and family law, and criminal defense in three Middle Tennessee office locations (Nashville, Murfreesboro, and Columbia, Tennessee).